Empowering Charity

Empowering Charity

A New Narrative of Philanthropy

Froswa' Booker-Drew

1845 BOOKS

Cover and book design by Kasey McBeath
Cover image courtesy of Unsplash/Jeffery Erhunse

The Library of Congress has cataloged this book under ISBN 978-1-4813-1609-5.
Library of Congress Control Number: 2022933280

CONTENTS

Part II
A New Model to Champion the Contributions
of Those Being Served

HERitage Giving Circle
Photograph provided by author.

"Philanthropy is commendable but it must not cause the philanthropist to overlook the circumstances of economic injustice which make philanthropy necessary . . . "

—Martin Luther King, Jr. (1929–1968)

ACKNOWLEDGMENTS

Writing is never done in complete isolation. If I did not have a community of support, this would have never happened. I am grateful for my family that offered space, affirmation, and even constructive criticism while I spent countless hours writing, reading, and researching.

The Holy Trinity—all three were ever-present on this journey—God, Jesus, and the Holy Spirit. I am grateful for the protection, love, light, insight, wisdom, and salvation given throughout this process and my entire life. I am nothing without your presence in my life. Continue to rain down on me and use me as a vessel to bless your people. Amen.

My daughter, Kazai, who is my heart walking outside of my body. I am blessed because I not only love this amazing human being, I respect her because of who she is as a woman. She is my thought partner, editor, and laughing buddy.

My mother, Dorothy, who is more than my mom. She is my confidante, friend, and collaborator. She pushes me. She reminds me of the "I am" in me.

Charles Drew—thank you. You have given me space, time, and support to do the things that matter. I am grateful for you more than you know. Your role in my life has gone beyond the title of spouse. You are a dear friend forever.

Pastor Chris Simmons and the Cornerstone Baptist Church family—thank you for more than a decade of love, knowledge, and support.

To my State Fair of Texas family—I am most appreciative of the opportunity to do work that makes a difference. Grateful for my team of rockstars to co-labor with in blessing lives, and co-workers who are passionate about creating memories for millions.

The Voices of Women—Shelly and the group—thank you for pouring into me and offering inspiration to know that God values my voice and my uniqueness through our weekly Zoom meetings. Thankful for these *ezers* in my life—Hebrew for "woman and warrior"!

To Nathaniel—thank you for your friendship, support, prayers, and encouragement even behind bars. You have been consistent in reminding me of the greatness within.

Esteria—thank you for sharing your family and especially allowing me to be a part of your journey with Chris. Losing that gentle giant has been painful but I know God is working in both of us to use that hurt for something special.

Personal Board of Directors—Dr. Terry Flowers, Greg Campbell, Barry Silverberg, June Holley, Michele Bobadilla, Dr. Harry Robinson, Dr. Karen Craddock, Dr. Constance Lacy, Comfort Brown, and many others—thank you for sowing into my life with your wisdom over the years, and to Zeb Strong, you are missed, my friend.

Baylor University Press—thank you for saying yes to my vision and believing in this dream to write a book that combines my faith, my passion, and my lived experiences.

To the South Dallas nonprofit community—so honored to be a part of your journey. I've learned so much from each of you and I am a much better person because of the opportunity I have to work with you.

My family—thank you! You are too numerous to name you all but I must say thank you to my aunt Theresa, uncle Mac, and cousins Kim, Debbie, Zena, Reggie, and Patricia, who always found the time to remind me of their love for me.

My Best Friends Forever—Shene, Lillian, and Deirdre—you have all been in my life since middle school and you haven't let go yet. I am grateful for your prayers, friendship, love, and sisterhood after all of these years. Thank you!

Prayer Partners and Friends—Cheryl W., Rahim S., Gaytha D., Shawana C., Candace T., Tammy J., Sherri M., Thana S.—thank you for the late nights of receiving my texts and standing in agreement with me.

Ladies of HERitage Giving Circle—I am honored to serve with such brilliant women who are committed to making a difference. Thank you, Akilah and Halima, for allowing me to join with you on a journey of building a legacy, a deep friendship, and a forever sisterhood.

If you were not listed, know that there was only so much room in these pages, but if you've ever played a role in my life as a friend, mentee, or colleague, I am grateful.

INTRODUCTION

When Akilah Wallace approached me about being a part of a giving circle, I became intrigued with the possibility but I thought it was out of my reach. I wasn't wealthy and the idea of being a philanthropist seemed removed from my reality. Looking back on our establishment and the impact we have made has been fulfilling. Who would have thought that a small group of women could make a difference with our time, talent, and treasure in such a short period? This is something that anyone with a passion and focus can do to make a difference.

A giving circle comprises a group of individuals who raise funds to donate to the organizations they identify and agree to support. Giving circles are usually made up of women but are not exclusive to women. Giving circles range in their areas of focus and can raise thousands of dollars, even into the hundreds of thousands. More and more giving circles, led by persons of color and women, are gaining traction. Giving has always existed in our communities, even when we have not been given the opportunity to speak into larger systems that control massive amounts of money. Our giving circle, HERitage, was formed by Akilah Wallace, who asked Dr. Halima Leak Francis and me to serve as cofounders. We formed the group to make sure that organizations led by Black women or serving a significant number of Black women and children could receive funding. We saw that many of these organizations are smaller grassroots entities that do not receive enormous support or visibility. Most of the women in our organization are in non-profit management at various levels (from entry-level to senior leadership) but other members are also attorneys, professors, consultants, and teachers. With more than forty members who donated either $500 or $1,000, we were able to raise $30,000 in our first year, which we donated to eight organizations. One of the donations was an in-kind donation of hygiene supplies for a nonprofit operating in a low-income apartment complex in a challenged community. In 2021, we donated more than $56,000![1]

Giving circles are not the only strategy for changing the narrative around giving, but they contribute to the move toward hope.

Philanthropy is steeped in myths that not only hurt communities of color but consist of models that do not work. Instead of relying on the social, human, and cultural capital of those in the community, we continue to employ a deficit-based model that will not change poverty. Until we debunk myths about poverty and philanthropy, things will not change. There is a solution, and it can have an impact at an individual and collective level. Many current philanthropic strategies have failed because they've neglected the experience, wisdom, and gifts of those receiving "help." A more effective model of philanthropy is one that champions the insights and strengths of those being served.

The Bible teaches that no person is unredeemable or helpless. I have found that media and many institutions project this false image. So often, in our group effort to live righteously and do the right thing, our acts of goodness are questionable. The intention might be to help but our motivation is often rooted in biased and harmful thinking. In this book, I will illuminate false narratives, discredit them with facts, and then provide tools and examples that can be implemented to change the trajectory of giving. Change will be achieved by giving those who are "helped" and with lived experience of poverty, positional power to make decisions and be a part of the process. We cannot continue to leave out the voices of those most impacted by philanthropy. Whether it is through board membership, program development, leadership in nonprofits, or charitable giving, the way in which nonprofits currently operate lacks inclusion. This is rooted in a belief of inadequacy: the notion that persons of color and the communities we come from are broken. This perception is inaccurate. People are not broken; the systems that are designed to help are broken, in need of evaluation and repair through our involvement and leadership.

As a Black woman working in philanthropy, I am blessed with the opportunity to see the other side of giving. I spend much of my time in a neglected area of Dallas, Texas, where the residents are often blamed for their condition. The lack of investment by both local government and the corporate sector has existed for decades. Despite the barriers faced due to racism and classism, I witness daily the dignity and resourcefulness of those who are perceived as needing help. Persons of color have found ways to survive amid oppression and obstacles. Historically, even with limited wealth, our communities have been committed to self-reliance and preservation. As a Black woman, I cannot speak for other communities. However, I recognize my limitations in speaking for an entire group, even the one I identify with. I can't. This book represents my opinion based on my lived experiences. I use "Black" and "African American" as descriptors, though I understand some people that are Black cannot trace their roots to Africa and some Black people are not American. I also use the term "BIPOC," which stands for Black, Indigenous, People of Color.[2] I believe definitions are important because they contribute to narratives. It is my desire to be respectful to those definitions.

There is a new narrative being created to change the false perception about underserved communities and communities of color, and it could change everything we thought we knew about giving, race, and class.

It is my desire through this book to amplify the stories of those who are often not at the table but are creating tables of their own to make a difference. I hope this book serves as a catalyst and a conversation starter beyond tolerance to work toward real inclusion in our workplaces, organizations, and communities. My desire is that this is a tool to develop strategies to make an impact for those we don't know, we don't see, or are viewed as "other."

Why We Need to Change the Narrative

Recently, a wealthy, White church in Dallas, Texas, purchased nine acres of land for $250,000. When they were asked what they will do with the property in this largely Black community, they replied that they were planning on bringing Jesus to the area (as if the community didn't already have Jesus! I think quite often we believe that poorer communities are less spiritual because of their environments and this isn't true).

Poverty is often seen as a result of dysfunction "inherent" in people of color. There are several myths that contribute to the belief that poverty is the fault of those who are poor: bad decision-making, laziness, no moral compass, or lack of a strong faith in God. If they only prayed or fasted more, things would be different. This narrative is faulty and damaging yet it has become a foundation for charitable acts. Giving allows us to feel as if we are making a difference in some way without truly exploring the real causes of the problem and instead focusing on temporary solutions. Legislative agendas often focus on temporary solutions to keep the public happy without addressing the real problem. This temporary focus is reflected in our voting practices, the policies we support, and even where we donate our money.

Though we wish to make a difference, our giving is targeted at causes that often do not touch on the real problem. Rather than dealing with the systems, bad policies, ineffective structures, and false information responsible for our social ills, donations provide band-aids to broken bones. We then blame those who limp along in pain because they did not heal as quickly as we needed them to. This is unrealistic and ineffective for the wounded and for those who think they are helping. Real change must combine funding with advocacy and narrative change. Many of these myths undergird the beliefs we have about the poor and play a considerable role in influencing philanthropic giving. This is why it is so important to examine and expose these myths. I will not only explore the myths but offer ways to "flip the myth" by changing the narrative and calling for action.

HARMFUL MYTHS ABOUT POVERTY, BIPOCs, AND PHILANTHROPY

Myths about Poverty

1

MYTH: POOR PEOPLE ARE LAZY

My grandmother, Mary McGaskey, worked hard. After two abusive and controlling marriages, she left central Louisiana in the early 1950s with my mother and uncle in tow and moved to northern Louisiana. My grandmother was not highly educated so she was only afforded the opportunity to be a maid. Even as a poor woman that lived in a shotgun house, with the help of her neighbors, her children were able to graduate from high school and start families. Her inability to finish school had nothing to do with intelligence. My grandmother's poverty had nothing to do with laziness. It was about the lack of opportunity.

Poverty is typically seen as an issue of laziness, poor money management, or bad decision-making. In 2014, news commentator Bill O'Reilly said: "You gotta look people in the eye and tell 'em they're irresponsible and lazy. And who's gonna wanna do that? Because that's what poverty is, ladies and gentlemen. In this country, you can succeed if you get educated and work hard. Period. Period."[1] While O'Reilly received a lot of feedback on his comment, he represents a whole line of thinking that poverty is the result of a poor work ethic. Often people imagine individuals who are not working and those who are taking advantage of the system and the generosity of others when they think of poverty. What people often fail to notice is the reality of the working poor: those like my grandmother, those who work multiple jobs with no benefits, those who are working for wages too low to thrive. According to the Brookings Institute, low-wage workers comprise most of the U.S. job force (44 percent), many of those are women and BIPOCs. Poverty is a much deeper issue than many people first imagine.

In our country, there is a common belief that hard work and effort are key to the elimination of poverty. This belief that if individuals work hard they will achieve success is called meritocracy. It does not, however, consider the impact of wealth and social class. People are not idle because they want to be; the issue is that they are not making enough money or do not have the skills to move into higher-paying jobs. In addition, challenges such as race and gender discrimination create barriers for mobility. Poor people in this country make less money and struggle just to make ends meet. The productivity rate in America has increased 77 percent since 1973 yet the hourly pay has only grown by 12 percent. If the federal minimum wage was based on productivity, it would be $20 an hour as opposed to the current $7.25 per hour. There are over forty-one million workers that earn less than $12 an hour, rarely with health insurance. This is a third of the workforce.[2] These people work hard yet they still live in poverty because the wage is unlivable.

In my work at the State Fair of Texas, I am a managing partner with Redemption Bridge, another nonprofit, to assist those who are impacted by incarceration find employment and livable wage jobs. There are over one hundred entities involved in this project, including local nonprofits in South Dallas and many departments within the City of Dallas, to assist those who are impacted by incarceration in finding employment. We have discovered that many of the individuals returning home from jails and prisons are unable to find work because of their backgrounds. It is not that this population is lazy. In 2020, "a staggering 27% of formerly incarcerated people don't have jobs."[3] State policies prevent this population from obtaining additional education during their sentence or after release. According to a 2020 Justice Center Council of State Governments report, more than forty states prevent formerly incarcerated educational opportunities due to offenses and sentence length.[4] This population deserves a chance. Preventing them from having opportunities to excel not only limits their God-given abilities, but it also hurts those who depend on them.

Many have used Christianity to promote the idea that poverty is related to a lack of effort. Proverbs 10:4 (NIV) states, "Lazy hands make for poverty, but diligent hands bring wealth." For most of my life, I've heard that poverty is equated to laziness and therefore it is a moral issue. The issue is that without paying attention to the barriers created by humanity through our biases and institutions, it is easy to misunderstand what impacts those who are impoverished. In a poll conducted by the *Washington Post* and Kaiser Family Foundation, "46 percent of all Christians said that a lack of effort is generally to blame for a person's poverty, compared with 29 percent of all non-Christians."[5] What is also interesting is that those who are poor statistically tend to believe in God at a higher level than those who tend to have more wealth.[6] Sixty-six percent of individuals who make less than $30,000 a year believe in God compared to 53 percent of those who make over $100,000 per year.[7]

It is a common belief that individuals are poor because of their sin versus the sinfulness of structures that are in place which contribute to and perpetuate poverty. Much of this is rooted in our interpretation of Scripture: "The soul of the sluggard craves and gets nothing, while the soul of the diligent is richly supplied" (Proverbs 13:4 ESV); "If anyone is not willing to work, let him not eat" (2 Thessalonians 3:10 ESV); "A slack hand causes poverty, but the hand of the diligent makes rich" (Proverbs 10:4 ESV). One Christian organization working in a predominately Black neighborhood posted on its website that poverty was the result of those who were sinful in their nature. Many Christians hold this belief. Derek Prince Ministries states, "If you are fighting poverty, if it seems to be oppressing you, check on your spiritual condition. See what is permitting that bandit to assault you and to move in on you and take you over."[8] This could be interpreted as "*Your lack of a relationship with God could be the reason you are poor.*" Our ideas about poverty are focused primarily on individuals and not the systems in place that cause discrimination, bias, and inequities in the distribution of resources.

This partial view of poverty not only informs our theology, but it informs our political discourse and policies that impact the poor. Politicians have also chimed in on the notion that poverty is a result of laziness. In 2014, Congressman Paul Ryan, commenting on the issue of poverty, confirmed the belief that laziness is the cause: "We have this tailspin of culture, in our inner cities in particular, of men not working and generations of men not even thinking about working or learning the value and the culture of work, and so there is a real cultural problem here that needs to be dealt with."[9]

In discussing poverty and even the role of philanthropy, we must use an equity lens for clarity. It is important to understand the difference between equity and equality. During the Civil Rights Movement, there was a push for equality because Black people were not being treated fairly. The same has occurred for women, Latinos, and other groups in this country who wanted justice. As much as equality is important, it can't be the sole focus. I wrote a piece in early 2019 for the Jewish Community Relations Council's Interfaith Seder that explains the difference.

In a conversation, someone compared equity to a team playing baseball for more than four hundred wins and then expecting the other team that hasn't had a chance to be in the game to catch up while the initial team continued to play. Equity is not a game that we view and go back to our respective spaces. It is about real people's lives. It is about creating access, resources, and opportunities for success. It is also recognizing the impact of privilege and power. Equality is defined as the state of being equal. If we are not careful, equality can exist in a state of fluidity, remaining a perception without real commitment, including policies and addressing/eliminating barriers that keep marginalized populations from experiencing true rights and opportunities. Equality does not address historical inequities. After the 1960s, laws were designed to create equality, and yet, for more than forty years, we can point to examples of the law not providing equality in many of our communities. Equity work is critical. It is about addressing why things happened, who it happened to, and rectifying those issues. Race is a significant factor in equity. According to the Center for Social Inclusion (now Race Forward), "When we achieve racial equity: people, including people of color, are owners, planners, and decision-makers in the systems that govern their lives."[10] Equity does not create wins for some and losses for others. Everyone wins when equity becomes a lens for all that we do.

When we examine poverty through an equity lens, we begin to see the lack of access many were denied for hundreds of years as it relates to obtaining wealth, owning property, or voting. Even with those strides, redistricting, gerrymandering, redlining, and other immoral practices were instituted to keep people of color out. It is also important to note that poverty involves many intersections of identity: race, gender, disability, and age. The goal is to demonstrate the poverty affects many and sometimes these identities are intertwined. What happens when a person is Black, female, disabled, and a senior citizen? An equity lens will allow us the opportunity to see each of these identities and what accompanies them.

When we think of the poor, we tend to envision young, able-bodied individuals, but this is a limited belief. The poor also includes populations who cannot work: the disabled and senior citizens. The Bible commands us to pay attention to these groups as well. In the Bible, Jesus has a conversation with his disciples about a man with a disability. In the Gospel of John, his disciples asked him, "Rabbi, why was this man born blind? Was it because of his own sins or his parents' sins?" "It was not because of his sins or his parents' sins," Jesus answered. "This happened so the power of God could be seen in him" (John 9:2-4 NIV). Just as the disciples saw this disability as something that was caused by sin, we too tend to believe that various conditions experienced in life such as disabilities are a result of sin. This causes society to neglect those who are disabled by not offering as many opportunities. Nearly four million people are living with a disability in poverty.[11] Our society also dismisses the role of our elders and their contributions to society. The Bible references this population and calls for us to value our seniors especially in a time of need. "Do not cast me off in the time of old age; forsake me not when my strength is spent" (Psalm 71:9 ESV). For senior citizens, the number of those in poverty is also depressing. Combined, these groups have nearly eleven million individuals who are in poverty. It has nothing to do with laziness or morality. In the community I work in, I find that many seniors do not have access to transportation, and the cost of quality and assisted living can be enormous. For seniors on fixed incomes, increasing rates of rent can exceed their monthly allotment, leaving little for food, medicine, and other needs. Social Security benefits are based on lifetime earnings. The less contributed, the less a person will receive. For those who may have worked in entry-level retail, hospitality, or trades like construction with limited access to 401(k)s and other benefits, Social Security is the only income available. That means that when seventy-year-old Marie goes to the grocery store or pharmacy, she must make a decision between paying rent or getting her medicine. Living expenses can exceed your retirement benefits.

It is actually very expensive to be poor, a BIPOC, disabled, or elderly. For instance, poor people are taxed in ways that most fail to recognize. According to the American Economic Association, "many of the poorest households who have cars pay as much as 2 to 3 percent of their income in gasoline taxes."[12] Those who are poor often travel further to work due to a lack of employment opportunities in their communities, which increases their commute time, expenses for gas, or need for public transportation. Public transportation is an issue in these communities because they are often underserved.[13] In South Dallas, I've been working with community leaders for four years to address public transportation in the area. Many residents must leave the area for jobs. At last, the transportation provider in the area will bring an existing service that accommodates many suburban areas which will now begin in Spring 2021 in South Dallas.[14] It took so much time and advocacy to make this a reality. In areas like the Inland Port, which is home to over thirty thousand jobs, transportation has been an issue for many seeking employment.[15] The establishment of the Southern Dallas County Inland Port Transportation Management Association[16] was critical because people who needed jobs were not able to get to the jobs because of a lack of transportation. The narrative could have easily remained that people were lazy and didn't want to work. The reality is that barriers exist which prevent these people from getting to opportunities, such as limited public transportation (which was initially designed for this population), money to pay for transportation, or a lack of access to cars.

In addition to the increase in expenses for gas and transportation, the poor also experience challenges and significant expenses in banking, healthcare, and food. Overdraft fees tend to hit the poor hard and, with the possibility of three overdraft charges per day, this can add to the expenses for a low-wage-earning family. Many of the poor are unbanked. According to an article in the Berkeley Economic Review, "In 2017, a survey conducted by the FDIC found that the number of unbanked households in the United States was 8.4 million, with an additional 24.2 million underbanked households, households that are not participating or have limited participation in traditional financial institutions."[17] Many of the poor utilize payday loans and cash checking services that take exorbitant fees: "The annual percentage rates for payday loans are between 300% and 600%"[18] but offer a longer time frame for repayment that compounds drastically.

Health care is also expensive for the poor. Research shows that people living in or near poverty have "disproportionately worse health outcomes and less access to health care than those who do not."[19] My pastor, Chris Simmons, of Cornerstone Baptist Church, often states, "That what begins as a $5 cold ends up being a $50,000 hospital bill" due to a lack of access to health care providers and the challenges that people of color have faced with health care providers. A friend's son in South Dallas contracted COVID-19 in college. He was hospitalized for months and had significant damage because of the disease. This twenty-one-year-old incurred a three-million-dollar bill for his care. He did not have insurance. Now that he is deceased, his family will deal with these expenses. As our country continues to deal with the aftermath of the pandemic, exorbitant medical expenses will create debt particularly for those who are Black and Brown frontline workers who contracted the disease. Low-wage workers do not have access to health or life insurance through their employers, and the fear of these expenses keeps individuals from seeking health care until it is too late.

Food deserts are another challenge for the poor. The USDA defines a food desert in relation to access, distance, and transportation to healthy foods at the store.[20] South Dallas is a food desert or, as some would call it, food apartheid. In many low-income communities, this state of affairs is intentional. I remember meeting with a grocer in our area to ask about the possibility of another store in the community. I was told that we had the "wrong rooftops." When I inquired more about this, I found out the real reason was that the area did not have individuals with disposable incomes. In poor communities, there are few options for healthy food and many use convenience stores to purchase food. In addition, those who are poor try strategies to make ends meet, including purchasing non-nutritious foods that will keep them full, or spreading out doses of medicine meant for daily use. Years ago, a friend, who we will call "Carrie," would purchase boxes of ramen noodles and popcorn to feed her three children so that they would not experience hunger pangs. She could buy more of those items because they were cheaper. Food insecurity is a setup for compounded health issues. As we focus on changing the narrative of philanthropy, we must be aware of the issues that plague individuals and communities that we desire to "help." Without an accurate understanding of our own biases, beliefs, and systems in place that cause harm, exacerbating the problem is inevitable.

Narrative Change: The myth that if you work hard the result will be a big payoff, in the end, is unrealistic for many Americans, especially for the working poor and seniors that have contributed to this country all their lives. The Children's Defense Fund states that "One in three African American, Hispanic and Native-American children live below the poverty line and one in 11 white children lives below the poverty line"[21] which means their parents are also poor. If we do not address the issues of race that are bound up in our conceptions of laziness as the root cause of poverty, it will continue to be easy for us to say that White people work harder and as a result, have more wealth. This is not true and once again does not tell the entire story of the impact of slavery, racial discrimination, and disparities in so many areas that contribute to this reality.

Neither laziness nor a broken moral character provides an accurate or complete explanation of the ongoing reality of poverty. Senior citizens who have contributed their life work in building this country may not be able to survive with limited financial resources. Those who are disabled are also impacted tremendously due to a lack of opportunities. We must consider various constraints that keep a person from fulfilling their dreams and God-given potential. Each person has value especially if we believe we are all created in the image of God and with purpose. The narrative change is that laziness has nothing to do with being poor or a bad Christian. Poverty is a result of a lack of opportunities, roadblocks the system creates, and several other outside forces. Poverty is rarely a result of something someone can control. Years ago, I remember visiting an exhibit that featured illustrations of five-year-old children noting what they wanted to become when they were adults. Every single child had an aspiration. I saw pictures of nurses, firefighters, and even stay-at-home moms. The events and environments that are faced between childhood and adulthood are the keys. Something happens that changes an optimistic, hopeful child for the future into one that becomes an impoverished adult. No one ever grows up with the desire to be poor or hungry. As people of faith, we must begin to recognize the role of trauma in our communities and begin to explore techniques to address this in our congregations and communities. "Trauma-informed care shifts the focus from 'What's wrong with you?' to 'What happened to you?'"[22] We must begin to understand what happens to people which starts with creating the space to listen to perspectives different than our own. Is there an opportunity to think about the narrative you have told yourself about poverty? What do you believe about the poor? There are many Scriptures that demonstrate God's heart for the poor. There are several below. Can you identify others?

Call to Action: Our theology must be challenged. Views about the poor are often attributable to our understandings of what the Bible says about wealth: that if you work hard, you will get rich, and if you are poor, then you are a failure as a person because you are either lazy or evil. This is both a misunderstanding of Scripture and an oversimplification of the harsh realities many people face. This theological correction should lead us to a correction of our social understanding: we need to recognize the various political and economic obstacles that exist to perpetuate the hardships endured by the marginalized.

The failure to consider the barriers that our society has in place that are stumbling blocks for many in our communities is apparent in the way we give. A lack of understanding, unwillingness to learn, and even a lack of empathy, create a skewed lens that does not allow for understanding contexts different than our own. In philanthropy, this is expressed in the way we believe money should be dispersed. Funds are given to those that are deemed as "deserving" and fit criteria based on an assessment of determined needs. The reality is that assessments and data can be limiting, preventing the full picture. This view is often from a perspective that fails to be inclusive of those who are most impacted. For most philanthropic organizations, funders are often White, male, over fifty, and have limited experience with poverty. Without a true understanding of the role of systemic or structural racism, classism, and gender, we are continuing to perpetuate a problem based on a false narrative.

According to a Citi report in 2020, "Systemic racism in the United States has had a huge cost to the economy: $16 trillion over the past two decades. That's the combined cost of disparities in wages, education, investment in black-owned businesses, and the housing market. . . . Present racial gaps in income, housing, education, business ownership and financing, and wealth are derived from centuries of bias and institutionalized segregation, producing not only societal, but also real economic losses."[23]

What are the possibilities for change in your community as we examine systemic racism and poverty? Many people believe incarnational ministry is one way of addressing poverty. This is to live amongst and contribute to those who are impoverished. The challenge in that theory is that, in our desire to make a difference, we could create more harm if we are not willing to unpack our biases regarding race, class, and gender. Sometimes the result of moving in can create an impact that we are unaware of such as gentrification or a missionary point of view to save others. Our job is to listen, to learn, and to bring others to the table who are often excluded from the conversation and the decision-making.

If poverty is not about laziness, then it must be a result of a lack of education. To have a seat at the table, the belief is education creates access. As a child, I was told that education was the key to economic success. This isn't the case for many in our society and is also another myth that must be debunked and will be discussed in the next chapter.

How do these Scriptures inform your thinking and action regarding the poor?

Psalm 14:6 (ESV): "You would shame the plans of the poor, but the Lord is his refuge."

Proverbs 19:1 (ESV): "Better is a poor man who walks in his integrity than a rich man who is crooked in his ways."

Luke 4:17-19 (NIV): "[Jesus] stood up to read, and the scroll of the prophet Isaiah was handed to him. Unrolling it, he found the place where it is written: 'The Spirit of the Lord is on me, because he has anointed me to proclaim good news to the poor. He has sent me to proclaim freedom for the prisoners and recovery of sight for the blind, to set the oppressed free, to proclaim the year of the Lord's favor.'"

Luke 6:20-21 (NIV): "Looking at his disciples, he said: 'Blessed are you who are poor, for yours is the kingdom of God. Blessed are you who hunger now, for you will be satisfied. Blessed are you who weep now, for you will laugh.'"

James 2:5 (NIV): "Listen, my dear brothers and sisters: Has not God chosen those who are poor in the eyes of the world to be rich in faith and to inherit the kingdom he promised those who love him?"

What does your faith say about the poor? Are your views in alignment with what the Word of God states?

2

MYTH: A COLLEGE DEGREE AND A JOB WILL SOLVE POVERTY

Since my father is a college graduate, I had no choice but to go to college. He was adamant that I could not take out loans for college. My father and mother worked hard to put me through school. I saw the many sacrifices they made by living well below what they had just to ensure that I could obtain that degree without being in debt. My father believed that it was his responsibility to ensure I had no barriers for my bachelor's degree. However, my master's degree was my responsibility. Even with a partial scholarship and working full time, while attending school full time, it wasn't enough to cover tuition and fees. I remember owing over $30,000 after graduating in the mid-1990s with a Master of Liberal Arts degree. It took years to pay off the debt I accumulated. Once again, I had to take out a loan to pursue my doctorate that I am still paying for. I'm fortunate because I'm older, with a more secure job, and can pay monthly on my debt. Incurred debt can become enervating for young people just starting their lives. I was fortunate because I didn't have the debt from my undergraduate degree compounded with graduate school. Many jobs today require advanced degrees and to have insurmountable debt, with everyday living expenses, is overwhelming.

The contribution of billionaire Robert Smith highlights the real challenge that many college graduates face.[1] In 2019, Smith donated thirty-four million dollars to pay off the loans of students at Morehouse College. For Black students, education is not the magical elixir for poverty. Upon graduating, the debt from college loans becomes debilitating for decades. For example, according to the Brookings Institute, the average white student loan borrower owes around $30,000; the average black borrower owes closer to $34,000. White borrowers pay down their education debt at a rate of 10% a year, compared with 4% for black borrowers. Nearly 38% of all black students who entered college in 2004 had defaulted on their student loans within 12 years, a rate more than three times higher than their white counterparts.[2]

I've seen this firsthand with many students that I've followed in my career in nonprofit management and education starting at St. Philip's School and Community Center in Dallas, an elementary Christian private school with mostly Black students.

Working at St. Philip's School and Community Center in the early 2000s was an amazing introduction to understanding the challenges that marginalized communities face. Dr. Terry Flowers, my former boss and mentor, helped me to learn so much about South Dallas, a community that like most urban neighborhoods was abandoned by the City, is now facing gentrification and the uprooting of families along with generations of history.

South Dallas is an area that has not received a lot of support from the city of Dallas in the past. Its zip codes represent some of the highest poverty areas of Dallas, and in addition, the zip code 75215 produces the second-highest number of incarcerated individuals in the state of Texas.[3] Eighty-four percent of the population is African American,[4] with a significant number of those individuals having median incomes for a family of four of less than $30,000.[5] There is a lack of infrastructure to deal with homelessness, limited quality housing, and schools that do not have the level of resources available to others that live in the northern part of the city. Even in this neighborhood that has suffered from over-policing, crime, and a lack of jobs, I saw families with mothers and fathers who worked daily. They struggled to take care of their families on blue-collar salaries.

Although I am back in South Dallas through my work at the State Fair of Texas more than a decade later, several things have not changed. Many believe that the poor are mostly single mothers who are a part of a generational cycle of poverty. We must recognize that there are two types of poor populations: those who may receive governmental support and those who don't. I have personally witnessed families with two parents who live on the margins. They make too much for governmental support and not enough to take care of their families. They live check to check without any assets and no savings. Many folks that are employed are just a paycheck away from losing everything due to the loss of a job, an illness, or a catastrophic event.

Asset poverty was defined in 1997 by Oliver and Shapiro: "A family is asset poor if its net worth is less than 25 percent of the poverty line for families of their size and composition. A family is asset poor if its liquid asset holdings are less than 25 percent of the poverty line for families of their size and composition."[6] In essence, if you do not have more than three months of your salary in savings or the ability to liquidate assets quickly you are asset poor. Even among those who work, some women and BIPOCs are still at risk of being one paycheck away from losing everything. According to the Bureau of Labor Statistics in 2017, "Women were more likely than men to be among the working poor. In addition, Blacks or African Americans and Hispanics or Latinos continued to be more than twice as likely as Whites and Asians to be among the working poor."[7]

Education is an equalizer for some and is considered a level of protection from poverty. However, it isn't necessarily the silver bullet to alleviate poverty especially with the increase of student loan debt for those who cannot afford to pay for college. "Among bachelor's degree recipients, roughly 3.6 million or 4.8% were living in poverty in 2017, according to the Census Bureau. That's up from 3.3 million and 4.5% in 2016."[8]

Even those with access to higher educational opportunities face significant challenges. For example, Brittany is a young low-income Black woman currently working on her PhD. She completed her master's degree at a local prestigious university that offered her a scholarship to attend graduate school. Despite receiving aid, Brittany has a difficult time paying rent even with part-time jobs. At one point, Brittany was facing eviction. Brittany is one of many college students that is poor despite the pursuit of advanced degrees. Our society correlates higher education with the creation of more opportunities and ultimately, wealth; however, for many students, the debt they will incur to survive while obtaining a degree will keep many impoverished.

It's not only the long-term impact of debt accumulation but short-term needs and a lack of resources that make it difficult for many students to even finish college. Several universities in North Texas and around the country have established food pantries for the students struggling to eat and pay bills while working towards their long-term goals. "Feeding America operates 316 pantries and 124 mobile pantry distributions on college campuses around the country."[9] Despite being highly educated, Brittany, as a college student, is a member of the working poor. She is single, with no children and yet, she struggles to live. Brittany, like many other students, experiences basic needs insecurity. A HOPE Center Study found out that of thirty-eight thousand students surveyed in both two- and four-year institutions, "58 percent were experiencing basic needs insecurity, meaning they lacked both food, housing and other needs."[10]

Years ago, I taught at a trade college, now defunct due to their admission and financial aid practices. My students were livid, especially those who were veterans, after they discovered that their credits would not transfer to other colleges in the area. Students were paying more than $40,000 for an associate degree! These for-profit colleges were convincing students of shorter lengths of time to obtain degrees without informing students of the amount of debt they will owe. Many of these for-profit colleges targeted students of color and women with the carrot of graduating quickly without disclosure regarding job opportunities, financial obligations, and transferability of credit hours. Although education is important, a real discussion is needed about student loans destroying the American Dream for many young people as they enter the workplace and making them vulnerable to poverty. The debt that many of these students will incur, compounded with interest will keep them impoverished despite the promises for upward social mobility as a result of the degree.

The belief that education and hard work are the solutions to poverty is only one part of the equation. This argument has severe implications in philanthropic circles. It becomes easy to victimize those who are poor and claim it is their fault that they did not pursue higher education or a higher-paying trade. These issues are then addressed incorrectly by directing funds to programs that provide job training without examining the availability of jobs in those fields. For example, there is an organization in our area that provides cell phone repair training for those in the community. There is nothing wrong with providing training. However, realistically, how many phone companies are hiring individuals to repair phones? What is more problematic is that the technology is changing so rapidly that what they are learning today may not be needed in six months. These programs celebrate graduating a class through the program but do not question how many have received livable wage jobs that are full-time with benefits. I hear often that more job training programs are needed and, if we are not careful, we continue to perpetuate the idea that the poor are not taking advantage of opportunities without examining training and educational offerings that are outdated or do not result in connections to real jobs. It is imperative to make sure that real opportunities are provided for those who take out loans for post-secondary education and that they are afforded the resources to pay the debt without losing everything in the process. This is not just about philanthropy. It's about examining policies that are harming communities and limiting how far our dollars could really go.

Narrative Change: We must change the narrative that obtaining an education is the magic bullet to alleviate poverty. It is important to recognize the role of debt for young people who do not have access to wealth and instead need student loans. My story is not the rule but often the exception. We cannot ignore the role that race and gender continue to play in the challenges that communities of color face as it relates to educational and employment opportunities that are sustainable with long-term impact. As we consider changes in philanthropic giving, it is important to not only recognize women, people of color, and the totality of their situations, but we must be included in the decision-making that solves issues.

Call to Action: Groups like SCORE,[11] a group of retired executives, provide their expertise to assist small business owners who can actually make a difference. Is there an opportunity to provide your expertise to a similar service in your community or to young adults on financial literacy, investing, or debt eradication? Can you offer your skills to help them identify job opportunities or build a business?

One of the ways in which your philanthropic dollars can change these statistics beyond issuing a check is using your skills to provide training with groups like Generation USA[12] or Year Up[13] that train young people for job opportunities. What does it look like to mobilize individuals to provide their expertise to make a difference as a mentor or coach dedicated to not just skill training but creating access to your network for opportunities? How is your organization, church, and community partnering to ensure that voices are heard not only in surveys but in creating space for actual conversations and proximity to solve these issues? Social capital, which is relationships, networks, and associations, is critical to bridging this gap. How can you use your social capital to make a difference for those who might not have access to relationships which can impact employment and educational opportunities?

In your community, what are available educational opportunities for those who are White and individuals of color? What are the barriers that are preventing student success for all students in your area? Is there an opportunity to become more involved in local educational advocacy organizations? Become familiar with groups such as Leadership for Educational Equity.[14] Organizations like Leadership ISD[15] have done a great job of educating citizens about local policy affecting students and schools. Does this type of entity exist in your community? Is there an opportunity to collaborate with these groups to create a new narrative around education? Get involved with StudentDebtCrisis.org to learn more about ways in which you can advocate around this issue.[16]

How do these Scriptures inform your thinking and action regarding debt and poverty?

Proverbs 22:26-27 (ESV): "Be not one of those who give pledges, who put up security for debts. If you have nothing with which to pay, why should your bed be taken from under you?"

Exodus 22:25-27 (ESV): "If you lend money to any of my people with you who is poor, you shall not be like a moneylender to him, and you shall not exact interest from him. If ever you take your neighbor's cloak in pledge, you shall return it to him before the sun goes down, for that is his only covering, and it is his cloak for his body; in what else shall he sleep? And if he cries to me, I will hear, for I am compassionate."

Exodus 22:25 (ESV): "If you lend money to any of my people with you who is poor, you shall not be like a moneylender to him, and you shall not exact interest from him."

3

MYTH: HOMELESS PEOPLE LIKE BEING HOMELESS

When I was fourteen years old, my house caught fire. I remember I was sick at school and my grandfather picked me up. As soon as we got to my grandparents' house, the phone rang. My neighbor called to tell him that our house was on fire. That was one of the most devastating and life-changing experiences for me. The fire started in the hallway and then spread to my room. My clothes not only suffered smoke damage, but the water from the fire hoses destroyed many of my items. I was thankful that the house wasn't completely engulfed but, as a teenager, it was so difficult knowing that we had to start over. My parents were raising me and my first cousin, and we moved in with our grandparents. My parents moved in with my uncle's family. I had a difficult time getting to school, and I ultimately had to move in with my parents because I had friends nearby that could drive me to school. After a few months, we moved back into our house even though, by today's standards, it wasn't the best living conditions. It rained into the house and there were other several issues but that's all we had. We didn't want to inconvenience relatives, and we made the best out of a bad situation.

A lot of Americans don't have that option. They can't move in with relatives or live in a hotel. A former hairdresser of mine was living with various friends and with her five children; she finally had no place to go and moved into a hotel. What she was paying weekly in rent was exorbitant, but she wasn't alone. When I would visit her, I saw many families living in the hotel while their kids played in the hallways. Even in my attempts to help, it was not enough money and food didn't last long.

The *Washington Post* featured an article in September 2019 exploring the growing problem of homelessness in the United States: "More than 550,000 Americans experience homelessness on a typical night, and 1.4 million will spend some time in a shelter in a given year."[1] For many nonprofits that service this population, the face of homelessness doesn't always display the struggles of those who are further marginalized because of gender, race, or status. It is proven through data that "men, black Americans, the mentally ill, domestic violence survivors, substance abusers, and veterans all experience homelessness at higher rates."[2] Age is also a factor. Several homeless people are above the age of fifty which increases the risk of becoming sick. Furthermore, there are more than two hundred thousand people who live outdoors who are not counted and even more who live in their cars. I see this across the street from my church. As the city pushed the homeless population away from the interstate, they moved into open lots in the community, creating a new set of problems including biohazards in the encampment they created.

For some reason, as a society, we believe that people who are homeless choose it as a lifestyle, made bad choices, or are simply lazy. This too goes back to the belief of meritocracy. In the article "Perceptions of Meritocracy in the Land of Opportunity," the authors state that meritocracy is embedded in American culture and that the United States is one of the only countries to believe that if you work hard and achieve, you will become wealthy. In many other parts of the world, success is tied to family wealth. In the United States, your family's background is tied to your education and economic mobility.[3] If your parents attended college, more than likely, you would attend college. You would be around individuals that are educated and have more resources because this is your social circle. Wealth in the United States is not solely contiguous on how hard a person works—you can work hard and still be broke.

Michael Young wrote *The Rise of Meritocracy* in 1958, which portrayed a futurist society that embraced intellect and merit instead of a society focused on social class. He became disappointed in how the book's premise became distorted by readers, and later in 2001, he expressed his discontent in the *Guardian*: "It is good sense to appoint individual people to jobs on their merit. It is the opposite when those who are judged to have merit of a particular kind harden into a new social class without room in it for others."[4] Have we dismissed a class of people because we have no room for them?

To believe that all homeless people want to be homeless is as much true as anyone who paints is automatically an artist. People are homeless for several reasons, and for many, it is a result of disasters—whether tornados or losing everything after all of one's savings have run out—and not a choice. "Homelessness is a symptom of a systemwide problem," said Claudia Solari, the author of the report who is now with the Urban Institute in Washington. "Society often blames the individual and sees homelessness as a personal problem, but this ignores the role that our social institutions play, such as not providing enough affordable housing."[5]

Recognizing that mental illness is indeed an issue, it is not the only factor that contributes to this growing epidemic in major cities and even rural communities. By making the culprit someone's mental health allows us to isolate their condition without examining the real circumstances that create the reasons why a person is homeless.

When I was a kid, my cousin, Ivan, was a firefighter. I remember going to his beautiful home to visit his family and my relatives. His place was the house for having fun during the holidays and family get-togethers. Ivan continued to grow in his role at the Fire Department. What started out as occasional weed smoking moved into heavy drug use. Ivan lost his job, his family, his house—he lost everything. For decades, he had been living under a bridge or in a shelter. His siblings always tried to help him get back on his feet or allow him to stay with them. Even in their desperate attempts to help him turn his life around, Ivan remained homeless. The impact this has had on his children and his immediate family was beyond just Ivan. I often wonder what happened to the Ivan who was once successful. What is really needed to help him and others who live on the streets? It is not that he wanted to live under a bridge. Not all the homeless have an addiction problem, however, it is an issue for many like my cousin. According to the Addiction Center, "Tragically, homelessness and addiction go hand in hand. The end result of homelessness is often substance abuse, and substance abuse often contributes to homelessness. The National Coalition for the Homeless has found that 38% of homeless people are alcohol dependent, and 26% are dependent on other harmful chemicals."[6] Many of those who are homeless also suffer from not only addiction but a mental illness, which is something we also noticed with Ivan. "HUD estimates that in 2019, 36% percent of the chronically homeless suffered from a chronic substance abuse problem, a severe mental illness, or both."[7]

The belief that if people can simply "get clean" is not that easy either. Treatment facilities often require insurance and out of pocket costs. Inpatient rehabs cost around $6,000 for a 30-day program while well-known centers cost up to $20,000 for a 30-day program. In 60- or 90-day programs, the total average of costs could range anywhere from $12,000 to $60,000.[8] Resources to cover these costs are limited and as this problem increases without serious intervention, we will see more people like Ivan on the street.

Ivan had bouts of being clean and, the last time I saw him, he was struggling to get his life together and stay clean. His life will never be the same. He's missed so much—births, deaths, and watching all of us become adults. We also missed out on his potential being realized. Further, we miss out on the potential and possibilities of all those who are impacted by homelessness.

The fix for homelessness can be viewed as a simple one—housing—and yet, there are so many complexities involved. Examining the work of organizations like Union Station Homeless Services is evident that this issue can be addressed through housing, advocacy, and relationship building. They have placed more than a thousand individuals into permanent housing.[9] The problem is that there is not enough housing available. According to *State of Homelessness 2020*,[10] temporary housing is limited and so is permanent housing. Although there has been growth in both temporary and permanent housing across the country, it is not enough. Transitional housing is a bigger challenge because it has decreased in the last several years. This means that there are not enough beds or time for individuals to build their lives, often placing them in a position to jump from place to place with no stability.

Homelessness directly costs each of us as well through taxes and human potential unrealized. The amount of money the healthcare and social system sustains is significant. In many cities and states across the country, funding for mental health and homelessness support has been reduced. The lack of access to these services results in an increase in emergency room visits. Individuals who are homeless utilize the emergency room at a greater rate than those who had permanent housing.[11] According to Green Doors, an organization that is committed to ending homelessness in Central Texas, homeless individuals "visit the emergency room five times per year."[12] Emergency room visits are expensive, and taxpayers ultimately absorb this cost. When we look past our views on meritocracy and commit to understanding the data, we can begin diverting funding to address the root causes of homelessness especially keeping in mind inequities that exist.

Narrative Change: The narrative change is that homelessness is not a choice but a complex issue that needs our human, social, and financial capital to address. I've never met an individual who enjoys being out in the elements of rain, snow, and extreme heat. Children do not aspire to be homeless when they grow up, something happens in their journey for homelessness to become a reality. We must identify those individuals in jeopardy of homelessness with solutions to prevent eviction, help those who are already experiencing it, and, as a society, work to solve it so that homelessness is not a reality in a country with as much wealth as the United States. Beyond donating Thanksgiving and Christmas meals each year, research and give to organizations who provide day-to-day support as well as those working towards systemic change to eradicate homelessness. As philanthropists, our dollars matter and so does our voice. It is important to use our voice as an advocate in the political process for change. Union Station Homeless Services in California has been successful by creating a community advocates program that partners homeless individuals with supporters who can walk with this population. They have also gathered individuals to speak at city council meetings to advocate on behalf of this community. Operating in isolation will not address this issue. One year, I received a grant application for additional funds to help the homeless. However, the applicant noted that they did not partner with other organizations. No one can do this work in isolation because it requires the collective power of information, resources, and relationships of many individuals and organizations to serve. As philanthropists, these are all things to consider when granting money or supporting organizations.

Call to Action: Several cities have implemented programs that allow the homeless to pick up trash and receive pay, like Los Angeles[13] and Little Rock.[14] These efforts are important, but our work must be rooted in partnerships with others that serve this population, in addition to housing, showers, food, and transportation that address the problem holistically. One of the challenges I see often in communities is the lack of asset mapping. Asset mapping is identifying the resources available in local communities that focus on what exists instead of highlighting the deficits. We assume that nothing is being done, and we reinvent the wheel without investigating what exists; where are the gaps and what are the opportunities to make a difference based on that information? As you think about addressing this issue or others and before writing a check, are there ways that you can bring your network or connect to others that can collaborate for impact? To learn more about asset mapping, visit chapter fourteen in the book to explore how this tool can help you find out more about what exists in your area.

How do these Scriptures inform your thinking and action regarding homelessness?

Matthew 8:20 (ESV): "And Jesus said to him, 'Foxes have holes, and birds of the air have nests, but the Son of Man has nowhere to lay his head.'"

Isaiah 58:7 (ESV): "Is it not to share your bread with the hungry and bring the homeless poor into your house; when you see the naked, to cover him, and not to hide yourself from your own flesh?"

Matthew 25:34-40 (ESV): "Then the King will say to those on his right, 'Come, you who are blessed by my Father, inherit the kingdom prepared for you from the foundation of the world. For I was hungry and you gave me food, I was thirsty and you gave me drink, I was a stranger and you welcomed me, I was naked and you clothed me, I was sick and you visited me, I was in prison and you came to me.' Then the righteous will answer him, saying, 'Lord, when did we see you hungry and feed you, or thirsty and give you drink? And when did we see you a stranger and welcome you, or naked and clothe you?' And the King will answer them, 'Truly, I say to you, as you did it to one of the least of these my brothers, you did it to me.'"

4
MYTH: WELFARE IS THE PROBLEM

When I was in college, a friend needed support. She applied for government assistance so that she could get help with buying groceries. As a college student, even with working a part-time job and some federal aid, she could not afford to buy food. She did not receive a lot of money and she definitely wasn't able to purchase steaks and lobster with the aid, as many may think. When we think of government assistance, we think of the stereotypical "welfare queen" portrayed in the media. The reality is that there will always be those that abuse the system, but it doesn't necessarily represent the entire group of people who need assistance to live.

The term "welfare queen" began with emphasizing the fraud of individuals like Linda Taylor. Taylor did scam the system repeatedly, but she was a criminal far beyond creating her multiple identities to cash in on government assistance. She was suspected of murder, kidnapping, and many other crimes throughout her lifetime. Yet, her life became the example for politicians, starting with Ronald Reagan, to target welfare without further examining the need for this program, once again using morality, race, gender, and poverty as the scapegoat for cutting and eliminating this program.

Individuals, such as the social scientist Charles Murray, have even stated that welfare is an issue of genetics: "You want to have a job training program for welfare mothers? Do you think that's going to cure the welfare problem? Well, when you construct that job training program and try to decide what jobs they might qualify for, you had better keep in mind that the mean IQ of welfare mothers is somewhere in the 80s, which means that you have certain limitations in what you're going to accomplish."[1] Murray believes that poor people, especially those that are Black and Brown, are genetically inferior to

White men. He stated that those who are poor are significantly less in their abilities than those who are above the poverty line.[2]

If the belief that welfare is being given to inferior individuals, our desire to support those who are less fortunate is then viewed as worthless and wasteful. It is imperative to understand the financial side of welfare and the amount families receive to live. The Center on Budget and Policy Priorities states that "the average SNAP recipient in 2017 receives $126 a month in assistance which is about $1.40 per meal."[3] SNAP benefits are for the elderly, single adults, and qualifying families to receive food. Years ago, I remember hearing about a mother with ten children who received over a thousand dollars a month for her family. Even if that were doubled, it wouldn't be considered fine living even with food stamps, medical, childcare, and housing covered for eleven individuals in a home. Food stamps do even not cover every item in the grocery store and some items require cash payment. At $1.40 per meal, many items that can be purchased are filled with salt, preservatives, and other items that aren't necessarily healthy.

In the last chapter, I briefly mentioned an experience that occurred in my twenties that really impacted me. I had a friend who married a man with three children he was raising alone. The children's birth mother left and did not want the responsibility of rearing her children. He ultimately abandoned my friend who was left to raise his children alone. I watched her try to purchase food, with no consistent support from either parent, for three children on her small income. She told me she would buy popcorn because it would keep them full. There were a lot of ramen noodles in the home because she could add mixed vegetables to it for a low cost. The addition of a $1.40 meal could have helped a bit, but it would not have created the impact that she wanted for her family or any family with multiple mouths to feed.

The number of individuals receiving assistance is not astronomical: "Only 23 percent of families living in poverty receive Temporary Assistance for Needy Families cash assistance in the United States."[4] Those on welfare do not spend money extravagantly as many believe. They spend less on food and entertainment as well as healthcare than those who do not receive government benefits.

In the book *Why Americans Hate Welfare: Race, Media, and the Politics of Antipoverty Policy* (1999), "Martin Gilens used empirical analysis to demonstrate that the visceral negative feelings evoked by 'safety net' and 'entitlement' programs link back to egregious misperceptions that these programs benefit only people of color."[5] African Americans and Hispanic Americans are not the sole recipients of welfare benefits as often portrayed in the media.[6] Contrary to popular belief, those who often need assistance are White and the working poor. More than half of the low-wage, fast-food employees receive government assistance.[7] These low-wage jobs do not provide enough income even in a full-time capacity for many to care for their families without additional support. Poverty has nothing to do with intelligence nor does being wealthy. Inheriting wealth does equate to the ability to keep it or the means to generate more. Everyone who is receiving aid isn't getting over on the system, these are just individuals who need support which is often temporary.

Narrative Change: Although there is welfare fraud, the vast majority of those receiving benefits are working, often have families, and are White. The argument posed by many politicians and social scientists that individuals receiving welfare are genetically inferior has assumed that most recipients are Black. This belief is inaccurate, rooted in bias and hate.

As we examine these myths that are embedded in our motivations for giving, philanthropy must examine its roots in giving. In early American history, one of the first philanthropic organizations was started by Benjamin Franklin, called Junto.[8] This was a group of twelve members of the intellectually elite in Philadelphia. Many organizations were birthed from this group, such as a hospital, university, and library. Meetings often included a list of questions that encouraged the pursuit of knowledge and networking, promoting intellectual elitism among wealthy White men. In the early years of the U.S. government, organizations were developed that addressed community needs but did not include the needs of women and people of color. The book *Beyond Tocqueville: Civil Society and the Social Capital Debate in Comparative Perspective*[9] makes the observation that private, voluntary associations solved social issues, unlike in Europe which was addressed by the government. Tocqueville, a French historian and social scientist, visited the United States and noted the rise of these associations. He saw that these organizations "challenged the moral authority of the government."[10] These organizations could determine what was important to focus on instead of the government deciding. He also warned that there could be a possibility of these organizations swaying public officials because they were representing the voice of the people. Journalist Albert Shaw in the nineteenth century began to track millionaires' charitable giving in the late 1800s, noticing that their wealth contributed to the establishment of schools and societies to help those less fortunate that did not include women and people of color as well as supporting institutions for cultural activities for the rich. The roots of modern philanthropy are based on the giving of wealthy, White males that did not aim to help women and people of color. Without this examination of the historical roots of philanthropy in America, we fail to acknowledge its lack of viewing others as equal, only as those who need help. It is also important to note that the establishment of these organizations was founded by those who were considered intellectually superior helping those who were perceived as less than. The goal was not to create equity or equality by empowering others with the same resources and knowledge to control their destinies. These roots and beliefs still influence philanthropy today.

Call to Action: Corporate social responsibility programs typically do not involve community members in their decision-making. Is there an opportunity within your company to create community advisory boards to ensure unique voices are at the table to speak into funding decisions? I would also strongly encourage foundations, churches, and nonprofits to make sure that boards are not just comprised of the wealthy but of those who can provide a different perspective about community issues and needs. As a philanthropist, begin to ask questions that hold organizations accountable to ensure that your dollars are going to organizations that have ethnic, cultural, economic, and geographic diversity. Ask about the makeup of not only their board and staff but also of their community partners.

How do these Scriptures inform your thinking and action regarding welfare?

Proverbs 19:17 (ESV): "Whoever is generous to the poor lends to the LORD, and he will repay him for his deed."

Proverbs 28:27 (ESV): "Whoever gives to the poor will not want, but he who hides his eyes will get many a curse."

Luke 14:13-14 (ESV): "But when you give a feast, invite the poor, the crippled, the lame, the blind, and you will be blessed, because they cannot repay you. For you will be repaid at the resurrection of the just."

5

MYTH: FOLLOWING THE RULES ENSURES SUCCESS

As a kid, I was told constantly that I had to be 100 percent better than my White colleagues to even have a chance. From the time I was in third grade until I graduated from high school, my classes were predominantly White. In high school, my graduating class was 269 people. Seventy-four were Black. In class, anytime something negative happened within the Black community, I was the representative to speak on behalf of the entire group. There was always this weight of showing up and being the best possible. Black folks have been taught that if we speak correctly, are highly educated, get a great job, and live in a wonderful neighborhood then we will be accepted into mainstream society. This concept of "respectability politics" has been handed down from generation to generation. If only we do everything correctly, we will fit in.

Respectability politics was coined by Evelyn Brooks Higginbotham in her book *Righteous Discontent: The Women's Movement in the Black Baptist Church, 1880–1920*. She shares the view of Black Baptist women who pushed the idea: if Black people behave well, acceptance was inevitable. For Higginbotham and many others of this era, "better" meant less violence, discrimination, hatred, and possibly more opportunities and inclusion. The reality is that even in attempts to incorporate religion, adhering to rules and regulations, and becoming educated, the attacks of racism did not stop.

This belief is an especially large part of Black women's lives. Changing one's appearance by straightening one's hair or altering communication is a form of behaving well for acceptance and survival, called code-switching. For many

BIPOCs and especially Black women, code-switching is an everyday reality. Code-switching was coined in 1958 by Einar Haugen[1] in his book that studied bilingual behavior. He noted that bilingual individuals mixed dialects or languages. It wasn't until the 1970s that George Ray connected bilingual behavior to Black's code-switching in language as well for professional success. When I was a kid, this was called speaking "proper": we talked one way at school but another way when we were at home or with family and friends.[2]

In a 2012 *Harvard Business Review* article, "Three Skills Every 21st-Century Manager Needs," the first skill listed for success is the ability to code-switch between cultures. For White people, it is a skill needed to understand for cross-cultural communication. For Black people, it is not just about interchanging English and African American Vernacular English.[3] Code-switching is still an issue for Blacks in America in the 2020s that impacts not only your professional mobility on the job, but it could mean life or death.

Ida Harris's article "Code-Switching Is Not Trying to Fit in to White Culture, It's Surviving"[4] notes how code-switching has become a part of our conversations with our children in dealing with the police. The conversation involves clear directives on how to switch up behavior when approached by police. It goes a little something like this:

"Turn down loud music."

"Adjust your posture."

"Keep your hands visible."

"Exercise good manners."

"Speak properly."

Such conversations are a response to the dominant culture's attitude toward Blackness as a whole. Unfortunately, for Black citizens, such a perverse attitude remains present during quite a few brushes with the law.

Lately, there has been significant coverage on police brutality in communities of color, especially within the Black community. There are endless examples of Black people who were following the rules who lost their lives.

- Sandra Bland, a graduate of Prairie View A&M University, was killed in 2016 allegedly by suicide after a traffic stop in Texas.

- Philando Castile was shot multiple times after informing the officer he had a gun during a traffic stop. He worked in a local school.

- Atatiana Jefferson was killed in her home after a neighbor called for a wellness check-in in 2019. She was a college graduate.

- Elijah McClain was an autistic, unarmed twenty-three-year-old man killed by police walking home after purchasing tea in Colorado.

- George Floyd was killed by police in Minneapolis, Minnesota for reportedly using a counterfeit $20.00 bill. For more than seven minutes, an officer kept his knee on his neck after Floyd repeatedly cried that he could not breathe, begging for his mother and his life.

I am a Black woman with a PhD, no record or arrests. I have dealt with being stopped by police several times and am searched often in the airport. When I was flying back to Dallas after one of my PhD residencies, one of my classmates, a White male, was appalled at my treatment in the airport. I was searched and he could not understand why. He was irate because he heard about this happening but did not believe it until he saw it happen to me. He thought I should have been even more distraught, but he did not realize that is a part of my existence in America. Having natural hair at one point would ensure that my hair would be searched when that was not the case for my Anglo friends who had ponytails or buns. Even when I have done everything right, I'm still subjected to searches. I remember flying to Toronto, Canada as a keynote speaker for a conference. I was searched and humiliated. I told the officers who searched me that having a PhD and being invited to speak in another country could not prevent me from experiencing detainment because of the color of my skin. It is frustrating when others minimize your reality without exploring that your experiences are your truth. You can do everything right and still be treated wrongly because of your race. Bias is real.

In February 2020, I was stopped driving a rental car in the same county where Sandra Bland was killed. The officer stopped me because I did not have a front license plate. When I explained it was a rental being returned the next day, he acknowledged he could tell it was a rental but said it was still my responsibility. I was then accused of drinking from a hand sanitizer bottle on the floor of the car. Then he asked why I needed a rental car, about my car at home, and why I did not drive it. I was not only livid about the line of questioning but was terrified for my life. After he checked my license, he returned with a citation and I drove away, shaking terribly and just glad to be alive. When I got home, I emailed the Office of the Inspector General as well as reached out to a friend who then connected me with leadership within the State of Texas. I received an apology for the behavior and ultimately began a friendship with a leader within the Texas Highway Patrol. However, this experience is unique. I was given the opportunity to share my concerns and express how many individuals who look like me do not have relationships that can assist with receiving answers.

For many, especially Black men who have had interactions with law enforcement, a traffic stop could result in death. The Stanford Open Policing Project data confirms that bias exists: "Officers generally stop black drivers at higher rates than white drivers." They found in nearly every jurisdiction, "stopped Black and Hispanic drivers are searched more often than White drivers." Kelsey Shoub, one of the authors of the book *Suspect Citizens: What 20 Million Traffic Stops Tell Us about Policing and Race*, stated, "'Driving while black' is very much a thing; it's everywhere and it's not just a North Carolina or a Southern problem but across the United States." Behaving well is obviously not the solution because behavior is not the problem, it is bias.

Narrative Change: So why is this important, especially in a book about philanthropy? We must understand that the rules that exist for some do not exist for all. Rules are applied differently depending upon biases, stereotypes, and privilege. In philanthropy, we apply standards that are often unfair when we don't understand how these rules affect the marginalized. As donors, we have unrealistic expectations that all nonprofits have access to the same resources, training, network, volunteers, and staff. We then punish those agencies instead of investing in their success. Advocacy is an important part of philanthropy as well. Organizations that advocate on behalf of marginalized communities need your support. As an ally, this doesn't mean taking over the narrative, but it means being comfortable with a narrative that is different than your own. Instead of dismissing or diminishing it, listen and challenge why you feel uncomfortable. I serve on the board of directors for a large, Christian nonprofit. At one meeting, another board member decided to pat me on the head to touch my hair. I was stunned. On day two of our board meeting, while I was seated, she stated, "I know this offends you, but I love to touch your hair." Even as I said no and stop, she did not believe she was doing anything wrong. She violated not only my personal space but did not care how I felt despite my demands for her to stop. She was not interested in how it made me feel but only in her fulfillment. This happens a lot in philanthropy. We often "do" to communities what feels good to us instead of respecting their needs or learning more about what's important to them.

Call to Action: In examining your community, think about the projects that have been recently developed "for" a population: the homeless, the mentally ill, or teens. Were those populations included in the decision-making in the project or programming? If you are a part of a nonprofit board, are both the client and community represented in the membership and if so, are those individuals truly engaged and included? When I walk into a room, I immediately notice if I am the only African American, woman, or person of color. For many of my White colleagues, this isn't even on their radar. How can you be more intentional in ensuring that diverse voices are in the rooms that you frequent?

How do these Scriptures inform your thinking and action regarding race?

Romans 10:12 (NIV): "There is no difference between Jew and Gentile—the same Lord is Lord of all and richly blesses all who call on him."

1 Corinthians 12:13 (NIV): "We were all baptized by one Spirit so as to form one body—whether Jews or Gentiles, slave or free—and we were all given the one Spirit to drink."

Revelation 7:9-10 (ESV): ". . . a great multitude that no one could number, from every nation, from all tribes and peoples and languages, standing before the throne and before the Lamb."

6

MYTH: BLACK, SINGLE, TEEN MOTHERS PERPETUATE POVERTY

When I was a sophomore in high school, one of my classmates was pregnant. She was a fifteen-year-old single, Black female. By most accounts, she was a contributor to the dominant narrative that single, Black mothers are the problem. For many, the belief is that in the Black community, the overwhelming majority of Black women have babies out of wedlock and that these women are predominantly teens.

Bill Cosby, in the 1990s, gave the infamous Pound Cake speech which solidified America's thinking that one of the many ills that plagued our country was the outbreak of pregnancy by Black women without husbands. Cosby stated, "No longer is a person embarrassed because they're pregnant without a husband. (clapping) No longer is a boy considered an embarrassment if he tries to run away from being the father of the unmarried child (clapping)."[1] In this speech, he blamed urban American culture for a lack of morals. Although this thinking is still prevalent, especially in many faith communities, it is imperative to challenge it with the facts.

In the 1990s, the number of teen pregnancies for Black people was significantly higher than the national average. Young Black women ages fifteen to nineteen had 116.2 births per 1,000 females in 1990, which dropped to 26.3 in 2018. For Latinas, in 1990, the births per 1,000 females were 100.3, which decreased to 26.7 in 2018.[2] Since the teen pregnancy rate has significantly decreased, and poverty is still a prevalent issue, it proves that this argument is outdated and inaccurate.

We must change this narrative about Black teen pregnancies with the truth. Since 2003, the number of births in women ages thirty to fifty-four increased while the number of births decreased for those younger than thirty. Although fertility rates were highest for Hispanic women in 2017, the group's rate has decreased by 27 percent, the greatest drop of all groups.[3] This is important to note for several reasons: older women are having babies more than younger women. Stereotypes about communities of color, particularly for Black and Brown communities, often emphasize high pregnancy rates yet there has been a significant decrease in the number of both groups.

Single mothers are often painted as the face of poverty, but the reality is that 54 percent of poor adult women are single and childless.

When I think of Mary, the mother of Jesus in the Bible, I often wonder how she would have been treated in today's environment. There is no mention of Joseph after the trip to Jerusalem to Passover when Jesus was twelve in Luke 2:41-52. Was it possible that Mary was alone in rearing Jesus and his siblings? Luke 2:52 (NIV) says, "And Jesus grew in wisdom and stature, and in favor with God and man." The community was obviously a huge part of everyday life for Christ growing up. Do we have the level of support for single mothers in our world that allows them to rear strong, God-fearing children? What can we do to advocate for and support these mothers and their children instead of blaming them for their condition?

Narrative Change: When I am conducting workshops, I often ask the audience to define poverty. The answers are all over the place. Some people will point to a lack of cash. Others will say it is a lack of access to resources. Some will discuss asset poverty—that people do not have more than three months of savings on hand to deal with an emergency. Others will point to spiritual poverty. We believe we know what poverty is, but our beliefs regarding what poverty is and the reality of poverty often do not match. Prior to reading the data in myth one, what were your thoughts about poverty? What has changed in your thinking since the reading? Having a shared language is important to make sure that we have the information we need to be properly informed, to create the change we'd like to see.

What we thought we knew about poverty is nuanced with variables not considered. The face of poverty has changed. Rather than being comprised of teen mothers, the composition of poverty is comprised of adult women, single, without children, and in several cases, highly educated. These women are not only African American but include all races. In philanthropy, there must be a concise, inclusive view of poverty that does not only focus on aiding individuals in escaping poverty but also on sustaining them as they build wealth and resources. Author and educator Eric Jensen has a comprehensive definition of poverty that examines various scenarios we don't often think about or categorize as poverty. Poverty can be situational due to a catastrophe, generational, urban, or rural which all have different contexts. In the glossary section, there are detailed definitions from Jensen for further exploration.

After reviewing the definitions of poverty in the glossary, think about your community. Who are the poor? How are you sure? Where are they and what is being done to address their needs? What can you do beyond writing a check or donating clothing/food that could make a difference?

Call to Action: It is important to consider these questions using both data and a biblical lens. Could the changes in the aforementioned numbers have something to do with the increase of educational opportunities for women of color? If education can contribute to opening doors to new information, networks, and opportunities, should our focus in philanthropy go beyond the band-aid of just pregnancy prevention to educational opportunities as an avenue for empowerment?

In Dallas County (Dallas, Texas), the community college district along with the school district has created a program called Dallas County Promise that targets students at low-income high schools to attend one of our local community colleges for free. Programs like Upward Bound are also great in providing college preparation for youth. What programs are in your area that help youth prepare for college or offer opportunities to attend college? Could your skills be used at one of the programs to teach classes, mentor, or introduce youth to other professionals in your network?

There are still teen mothers that need our help. Television shows like *Unexpected* on the Discovery Channel Network provide a realistic view of what teen parents experience. How can you support organizations like Viola's House,[4] Lullaby House,[5] or I Look Like Love,[6] Bridges Safehouse,[7] and Carter's House[8] that help teen and single mothers with housing or clothing? Find out if there are organizations similar to this in your area. They can use volunteers to help with holding babies, running errands for mothers, mentoring, or administrative help. Even many local hospitals seek volunteers to help in neonatal units. Is this an opportunity to give back and demonstrate love as we are commanded to do?

How do these Scriptures inform your thinking and action regarding single or teen mothers?

Psalm 68:5 (ESV): "Father of the fatherless and protector of widows is God in his holy habitation."

Exodus 22:22-24 (ESV): "You shall not mistreat any widow or fatherless child. If you do mistreat them, and they cry out to me, I will surely hear their cry, and my wrath will burn, and I will kill you with the sword, and your wives shall become widows and your children fatherless."

Romans 8:1-5 (ESV): "There is therefore now no condemnation for those who are in Christ Jesus. For the law of the Spirit of life has set you free in Christ Jesus from the law of sin and death. For God has done what the law, weakened by the flesh, could not do. By sending his own Son in the likeness of sinful flesh and for sin, he condemned sin in the flesh, in order that the righteous requirement of the law might be fulfilled in us, who walk not according to the flesh but according to the Spirit. For those who live according to the flesh set their minds on the things of the flesh, but those who live according to the Spirit set their minds on the things of the Spirit."

7

MYTH: BLACK FATHERS ARE ABSENTEE DADS

My parents defy all stereotypes about Black marriages. Dorothy and Willie married, divorced, remarried one another, and stayed together until my dad passed away at the age of fifty-six in 2005. My dad's parents were also instrumental in my life. My grandfather, Louis, and grandmother, Thelma, were married more than fifty years until PawPaw passed away in his seventies when I was nineteen years old. I always saw Black marriages. I grew up witnessing Black couples who were committed to one another and raising their children even if they decided not to remain together. One of the most amazing fathers I personally witnessed was a Black, single dad who raised his son from the time he was eighteen months old until he became an adult without any help from the mother. Many Black fathers I know personally are heavily involved in their children's lives.

Black fathers are in their children's lives even if they are not married to the mothers or live with them. Data from the Centers for Disease Control in 2013 illustrates that Black fathers are involved in the lives of their children more than we have been led to believe.

- Did you know that Black fathers prepared or ate meals more with their children versus their white and Hispanic counterparts with their children under the age of five?

- Did you know that Black fathers took their children between the ages of five and eighteen to and from daily activities more than their white and Hispanic counterparts?

- Did you know that Black fathers also helped their kids with homework more than their white and Hispanic counterparts?[1]

It is important to examine the multiple reasons that may prevent Black fathers from being as involved in their children's lives. It is not an issue of a lack of commitment but other variables such as incarceration that serve as a barrier. Incarceration for Black men (and women) is significantly higher than in most groups. Dr. Ashley Nellis wrote an article entitled "The Color of Injustice: Racial and Ethnic Disparities in State Prisons," where she states, "In eleven states, at least 1 in 20 adult black males is in prison. In Oklahoma, the state with the highest overall black incarceration rates, 1 in 15 black males ages 18 and older is in prison. African Americans are incarcerated in state prisons at a rate that is 5.1 times the imprisonment of whites." It is not that African American males are committing more crimes despite what we see on the evening news. Statistics demonstrate that Black people are overrepresented in the criminal justice system and are sentenced longer and harsher than whites for the same crimes. It is a justice system that penalizes Black people at a greater rate than other groups.[2]

I have a dear friend who is incarcerated and despite his sentence, he maintains contact with his daughter through phone calls, letters, and visits. He received a twenty-year sentence for a first-time, nonviolent, non-drug-related offense. Keep in mind that there are individuals who commit multiple crimes and received less time because of their race. For example, Johnathan Alger Moore, a white male in his thirties, has a lengthy criminal history including five DWI convictions. Days after one of his many releases, he drove drunk and killed a Dallas councilwoman and her daughter.[3] Sentencing is not consistent and is often biased based on race and gender. The report *Demographic Differences in Sentencing: An Update to the 2012 Booker Report* confirms that my friend's situation is not unique and happens regularly: "Black male offenders continued to receive longer sentences than similarly situated White male offenders." Despite the unfair conviction rate for Black people in the criminal justice system, my friend's limited ability to be present for his daughter has not stopped his tenacity to find ways to remain connected to her. Through the support of friends and family, he can talk with her consistently, even helping with homework over the phone. This is not the case for everyone, and the amount of money spent by family and friends for calls can be prohibitive for most families, often hindering contact.

The implications for incarceration are significant. The amount of money the United States spends on incarcerating Black men and women is in the billions. Yahoo Finance conducted an analysis which found that

> Americans have shelled out a staggering $4.12 billion to incarcerate innocent men and women since 1989 . . . Black men make up the majority of those wrongfully convicted—approximately 49%. And since

1989, taxpayers have wasted $944 million to incarcerate Black men and women that were later found to be innocent. That number climbs to $1.2 billion when including Hispanic men and women.[4]

Wrongful incarceration is expensive on several levels. The cost is more than trials and incarceration. When we account for time lost with children, financial, emotional, and physical support, the loss to both the economy and the lives of future generations is astounding. According to the report *Parents Behind Bars*, 99 percent of incarcerated men are fathers.[5] Consider the challenges those fathers face when they are required to check a box to indicate their criminal history and the barriers they face for employment and housing which in turn limits their ability to support their families. It creates a revolving door that could be resolved if this system was changed. Shows like *Maury* exacerbate the perception that Black men are making babies with no commitment or care. The shattering reality is that Black men are involved and for many, the injustice of the justice system makes it more difficult to be present and active parents. This is important to note because so often it is easy to believe that these fathers do not care or are not involved. There are barriers that create their full engagement both when they are in prison and when they return home.

Narrative Change: Not all Black men are absentee fathers or the noncommittal men we see on reality shows. We must consider the impact of incarceration as a contributor to generational poverty, especially when sentencing is not fair, is longer, and continues far beyond time served. Overwhelmingly, philanthropy is often dedicated to supporting causes that affect women and children but not inclusive of programming that champions the needs and successes of men of color. As you think about your community, how are Black men perceived? What is being done to address reentry in your area? The story of Stanley Andrisse is one that is a model for change. Andrisse was incarcerated for ten years. Behind bars, he began college courses and continued upon his release. He now has a PhD, teaching at John Hopkins and Howard University as a scientist. The founder of From Prison Cells to PhDs, he works tirelessly to help others obtain higher education while behind bars. If we look at the amount we spend on incarceration compared to the price of college education, we are wasting money as a country. Instead, there are many programs like his that can rehabilitate those who can be influenced positively for change. Are there programs in your area like the reading program for inmates in Seattle that ensure literacy and connection between parents and inmates?[6] What would this look like in your community?

Call to Action: As a society, those impacted by incarceration are not usually on the top of the priority list to fund. For those organizations that are providing reentry services, they usually have less visibility and struggle to fund their work. Are there opportunities in your community to not only support these organizations financially but assist with building their capacity? Currently, I am working with our local United Way to continue the Nonprofit Infrastructure Initiative. For the first two years, we focused on providing training, technical assistance, coaching, and leadership circles for grassroots nonprofits. In our third year, I conducted training on change management and network weaving so that they could think strategically about collaboration. In 2020, we focused solely on organizations in the reentry space.

Could you partner with the Amachi program of Big Brothers Big Sisters to make sure that children with incarcerated parents have a mentor? One in twenty-eight children have a parent that is incarcerated.[7] Children of incarcerated parents are three times more likely than children without parents in jail to go to prison.[8]

As philanthropists, our roles are more than just donating money. How can you advocate to ban the box (a movement dedicated to removing the box on applications that indicates if a person was in prison)? If one has completed their time, one should not be penalized again. This creates difficulty for individuals to get jobs or housing, placing them at risk of violating probation or parole if they are unable to obtain gainful employment on a local and statewide level. Here are several ways to advocate for change that can impact those impacted by incarceration and their families:

- Restore Pell Grant eligibility for all incarcerated students. Learn more about the REAL Act (S. 1074, H.R. 2168) or the Second Chance Pell Grant Program.

- Remove questions regarding criminal history from college admission applications. Currently, Beyond the Box for Higher Education Act (S. 1338, HR. 2563).

- Support the Office of Correctional Education to standardize educational programming within the Bureau of Prisons through vetting and quality control oversight. Currently, PREP Act (S. 1337, HR. 2635).

- Support organizations like Prison2Professionals, Prison Entrepreneurship Program, and Miles of Freedom, along with many others that are working in this space as well, encouraging funders to contribute to these and fatherhood initiatives.

- Investigate initiatives like Clean Slate as an option in your area for those impacted by incarceration at https://www .americanprogress.org/issues/poverty/reports/2018/11/15/ 460907/clean-slate-toolkit/.

One of the most important things that donors must realize is the role of advocacy. So many policies have been created that are detrimental to the poor and marginalized. How can you as a donor use your networks, finances, and voice to make a change in partnership with those who are impacted? It isn't that people need you to speak for them. They need platforms and partnerships to share their stories. How can you do that? Think about what your money supports through your local bank. Ask your bank or financial planner how your funds are invested and if those funds are supporting mass incarceration.

How do these Scriptures inform your thinking and action regarding those who have been incarcerated?

I think as believers, we must remember that many of those we celebrate in the Bible were arrested or imprisoned:

- Joseph went to jail. (Genesis 39:19-21)
- Samson was imprisoned by the Philistines. (Judges 16:21-23)
- Jeremiah was cast into prison because of his prophecy. (Jeremiah 32)
- Daniel was arrested and thrown into the pit of lions. (Daniel 6:16-28)
- John the Baptist was put in prison. (Matthew 14)
- Jesus was arrested. (John 18)
- Paul was in jail with Silas. (Acts 16:25-31) (Paul was in jail multiple times)
- Peter was placed in prison. (Acts 12)

Hebrews 13:3 (ESV): "Remember those who are in prison, as though in prison with them, and those who are mistreated, since you also are in the body."

Matthew 25:36 (ESV): "I was naked and you clothed me, I was sick and you visited me, I was in prison and you came to me."

Psalm 69:33 (ESV): "For the LORD hears the needy and does not despise his own people who are prisoners."

MYTHS ABOUT BIPOCs AND PHILANTHROPY

My story is just one of many individuals who are using their networks, finances, and expertise to create an impact in an environment that has not always been inclusive of donors of color. There are several myths that exist about people of color in philanthropy. This section is designed to dispel those myths and offer facts about the current movement of new voices in this space.

8
MYTH: BIPOCs DO NOT GIVE

There is a perception that Black folks are not charitable and active in their communities. From a perusal of the standard literature on American history, it could seem like Black communities have largely been uninvolved in the improvement of their surrounding communities which is inaccurate and misleading. W. K. Kellogg Foundation (WKKF)'s report *Cultures of Giving: Energizing and Expanding Philanthropy by and for Communities of Colors* states that African Americans give away 25 percent more of their income per year than whites.[1] We are often seen as needy and overdependent on government support. And even though we give, many of us do not see ourselves as philanthropists. As a child, I saw my parents in Shreveport, Louisiana helping others. At the time, I didn't realize that the trips to visit the sick, the donations to those in need, or even delivering cooked meals, were part of philanthropy in my community. I'll never forget watching my dad give meals to homeless individuals who were outside of our family restaurant. He would give them a task to complete because he believed in never stripping people of their dignity. At the end of the task, he would give them a hearty meal—no charge. My involvement in service began volunteering as a teen and has not stopped. I first volunteered at the Life Science Museum a few miles from my house when I thought medicine would become my career (thank God that changed!). My first job in college was a result of volunteering. I was Assistant Director for Texas A&M's Dallas outreach office in partnership with three universities to help first-generation college students see higher education as an option. I did not realize that providing workshops on diversity to high school students would have opened the door to my work in nonprofit management. I have made a life of giving. I now call myself a philanthropist, something I would not have called myself years ago because I did not realize that, like my parents, I was a part of this work.

I discovered in my nonprofit career that few foundations support organizations of color. Foundations also often focus on narratives of brokenness, instead of supporting organizations that are already community assets (per Understandtogether.com, "resources which individuals and communities have at their disposal; those which can be leveraged to develop effective solutions to promote social inclusion and improve the health and well-being of citizens"[2]) but may not have everything on the checklist to get approved for funding.

My involvement in philanthropy became more focused by connecting to Tracey Webb, the founder of the now defunct blog, Blackgivesback.com. In this blog, Tracey offered a glimpse into everyday individuals' lives who were making a difference through their giving. I had the pleasure of writing for the blog for several years, which strengthened my awareness of the impact of black philanthropy. This opportunity exposed me to the work of Akira Barclay, a renowned author exploring Black philanthropy. She, too, was a writer for the blog.

Working with Tracey introduced me to the idea of giving circles. Tracey started Black Benefactors,[3] a giving circle based in Washington, DC, and was wildly successful at bringing a group of Black professionals together to donate not just money but time and talent to Black causes and leadership. In 2018, Black Benefactors made grants to The Black Swan Academy[4] and Scholarchips,[5] two important organizations working in the DC community to enhance youth opportunities, even for the most marginalized.

I was further inspired by Black women's philanthropy after learning about another African American Women's Giving Circle in DC.[6] Watching the success they had in supporting causes for Black women and girls encouraged me immensely. Black Philanthropy Month[7] was also something that inspired me to get more involved in the space of Black giving. Black Philanthropy Month occurs in August each year designed to highlight philanthropists and organizations led by Black people.

Ultimately, a documentary called The Contradictions of Fair Hope,[8] which won the best long documentary at the Newark Black Film Festival's Paul Robeson Awards also reeled me into the world of Black giving. The film provides an example of Black giving by highlighting the Fair Hope Society in Alabama. Formed by freed slaves in 1888, the Fair Hope society helped those most in need: the sick, the hungry, and those who had lost a loved one and needed funds for burial. The society worked as a form of insurance, where members paid ten cents a month to be entitled to the services, and leftover funds went toward a yearly celebration. These societies around the United States, like Fair Hope and that Black giving, were and still are a huge part of the Black Experience in America.

When Akilah Wallace,[9] the founder of the HERitage Giving Circle, approached me and Dr. Halima Leak Francis to play a part in creating the first Black Women's Giving Circle in Texas, I was reminded of our legacy and wanted to be part of something even more powerful for the future. HERitage Giving Fund[10] was founded in August 2017, during Black History Month. The mission of the HERitage Giving Fund is to encourage philanthropy in the African American/Black community in a strategic and meaningful way and to bring a new source of funding to nonprofit organizations serving African American women and girls throughout North Texas. This organization has made philanthropy accessible for those who never thought of themselves as philanthropists and continues to highlight the past, present, and future of Black giving.

Brooch for HERitage Giving Circle members
Designed by Dr. Halima Leak Francis.
Photograph provided by author.

HERitage is committed to engaging Black women of varying economic status and backgrounds, who have a heart for investing in organizations, often grassroots, or startups. These organizations typically have limited access to the funding sources needed to support basic operating needs (staff income, supplies, transportation, etc.). We help increase service capacity and reach and sustain much-needed program services over time. This is just one reason why Heritage Giving Fund and other giving circles are so important.

The HERitage Giving Fund awards grants to organizations located in North Texas, led by Black women, using a lens sensitive to gender to frame strategies, and have a sound mission and objectives for impact. HERitage Giving Fund also serves as a hub for social events and discussions on how to build empowerment through philanthropy.

I serve as a founding officer and grants committee chair. In 2018, we raised almost thirty thousand that was awarded to eight organizations that are led by women of color as executive directors, board chairs, or program directors. In 2020, we dispersed funding to organizations to use during COVID-19 that has resulted in a total of fifty thousand in the last three years for nonprofits led by Black women. In 2021, we were able to donate more than fifty-six thousand to organizations in our area as a result of our donations along with friends and allies. It has been amazing to work with a group of women who are so committed to their local community. It is even more impressive that these community role models use their resources to continue this rich legacy of giving. Groups like HERitage are one of many examples of giving in Black communities and other communities of color that are crucial to America's future, inspired by the past.

Narrative Change: Black people, like many communities of color, despite some of the challenges we face, are involved in community building and giving. As a Black female, I've witnessed giving in my community my entire life. HERitage is an extension of what I saw women doing as a kid in the church through the mission programming. There are many giving circles that have developed since our establishment. Orchid was the first giving circle in our area which focuses on Asian women. They have been leaders in philanthropy and instrumental in serving as a catalyst of HERitage and other circles that followed. The other giving circles in the Dallas area that are housed in the Texas Women's Foundation include The Village, a Black women's giving circle, that provides funding for organizations serving the Black community, and H100, a giving circle of Latinas providing support to organizations that impact the Latinx community.

BIPOCs have a history of giving. Despite the barriers, it did not stop us from making a difference through philanthropy. The Urban Institute's blog on philanthropy provides information about giving in Black communities. Even with less generational wealth, giving is a part of who we are. The blog states, "From a historical and institutional perspective, Black communities have robust networks and organizations that support and facilitate charitable giving and help maintain high levels of charitable participation. Black communities have some of the oldest and most deeply entrenched identity-based funds (e.g., Black United Funds, foundations affiliated with civic and fraternal organizations, and giving circles) that are created, led, and supported by community members."[11]

Call to Action: Starting a giving circle isn't complicated. What is an issue that you are passionate about? The women in my giving circle and I knew we were passionate about supporting Black female-led organizations that were making a difference in the community. We soon realized that these organizations did not have the visibility or support because they are usually small and grassroots. When we began our giving circle, Akilah worked for Dallas Women's Foundation (now Texas Women's Foundation) who were instrumental in guiding us through the process. Our fund was initially housed at the Foundation. Since they hosted the fund by providing support in the formation through offering a website hosting including the grant application and writing the checks to the organizations, there is an administrative fee. From there, the three of us developed the mission and focus, selected the logo, and brought our friends together to share the idea. We had several mixers and gatherings to share our vision. Founding members had the opportunity to pledge $1,000 which gave them voting privileges when we selected the organizations. Those who donated $500 could not vote but were included in all of our events and the grant process. Members were given the option to pay monthly. We received reports monthly regarding donations.

After we created the criteria for funding, we worked closely with the Foundation to develop our application. We held in-person events to walk local organizations through the grant application and process. We also held a technical assistance call to answer questions. When the portal closed, our grant committee that I led received a list of applicants from the foundation that met the criteria for funding and submitted a completed application. Members were assigned to on-site visits. The visits were an opportunity to learn more about the organization based on an application the reviewer completed and scored. The site visit reports were compiled with the applications. Paid members voted and decided on the organizations that received funding. In year one, seven organizations received funds, and one received hygiene products for the young women they serve. We hosted a check ceremony for the winners to honor them and recognize our members. We spent 2019 raising funds to distribute for 2020. Our fund is now housed with Moore Philanthropy,[12] based in Colorado and New York.

I had the pleasure in May 2020 of moderating a conference sponsored by Philanthropy Together. Prior to that, I was unaware that this global organization is committed to helping individuals start giving circles and supporting existing circles. Philanthropy Together is a "new nonprofit, co-created by hundreds of giving circle and collective giving network leaders, to help start new giving circles and help existing giving circles thrive. . . . a global movement to diversify and democratize philanthropy."[13] This is a great resource if you are interested in starting a giving circle. There are many ways to do this work and HERitage is just one example. With some of the information I shared about our experience with starting HERitage, is this something that you can do with your friends or colleagues to make a difference in your community?

How do these Scriptures inform your thinking and action regarding giving?

Luke 6:38 (ESV): "Give, and it will be given to you. Good measure, pressed down, shaken together, running over, will be put into your lap. For with the measure you use it will be measured back to you."

2 Corinthians 9:7 (ESV): "Each one must give as he has decided in his heart, not reluctantly or under compulsion, for God loves a cheerful giver."

1 Timothy 6:17-19 (ESV): "As for the rich in this present age, charge them not to be haughty, nor to set their hopes on the uncertainty of riches, but on God, who richly provides us with everything to enjoy. They are to do good, to be rich in good works, to be generous and ready to share, thus storing up treasure for themselves as a good foundation for the future, so that they may take hold of that which is truly life."

9

MYTH: BIPOCs DO NOT HAVE A HISTORY OF GIVING

Working at St. Philip's School and Community Center was instrumental in my growth during my thirties. I developed my skills in building programs and relationships in a marginalized community. I also saw many affluent families bring their children to the school because of the education it offered and the proximity to the Black community in South Dallas. For many in the Black community, it's important not to forget your roots and the struggles that so many face. St. Philip's location and partnerships provide awareness of and access to cultural events and institutions such as the African American Museum of Dallas, the South Dallas Cultural Center, or the homes (now museums) of Kathlyn Joy Gilliam and Juanita Craft. It was important for me to make sure that when my daughter was young (she's now a junior in college) to see Black doctors, attorneys, educators, and other professionals to know that Black wealth does exist. I have learned that you can't be what you don't see. Exposure can make a significant difference. Several of her friends lived in Frost Farms, a beautiful area of homes in a suburb of Dallas that start at $350,000 to over $1 million with many Black home-owners. Despite the significant poverty that many face in our communities, Black and Latinx millionaires exist.

Black giving is a part of American history. Bishop Richard Allen was the founder of the African Methodist Episcopal Church in 1794. He and Absalom Jones founded the Free African Society that provided aid to freed slaves. One of the most famous millionaires and philanthropists was Madame C. J. Walker. She transformed the lives of Black women through the development of black hair care products. Mainstream cosmetic companies did not target or create products for Black women because they did not realize the demand and need in this market. Walker trained other women in how to sell the product around the country, creating jobs and income opportunities. Her estate was estimated at $600,000 at her death which is reported to be the equivalent of $8 million dollars today. She learned from Annie Malone, who was another Black female millionaire creating hair care products for Black women. Walker was committed to making a difference by giving money to several causes that impacted the Black community during her lifetime. Walker's financial success mobilized Black women to become entrepreneurs, and along with her charitable giving, has memorialized her legacy today.

Even after the death of Madame CJ Walker, pockets of wealth have existed in the Black community. There is a growing body of research that demonstrates that high net worth donors of colors are more prevalent than realized. According to the 2017 report *The Apparitional Donor: Understanding and Engaging High Net Worth Donors of Color*, "People of color (Note: People of Color comprises all groups that are non-White) collectively made up 23–24% of all millionaires in the United States, or between 993,000 and 1,039,000 persons. In 2013, 8% of Africans, 8% of Asians, and 7% of Latinos were millionaires."[1] Data from this report "reveals nearly two million African American, Latino, and Asian households with more than $500,000 in household wealth."[2]

Gender doesn't limit giving, either. Women of color are very generous according to the 2019 report *Women Give 2019: Gender and Giving across Communities of Color*. Several gaps were identified in the research for donors of color: "Minority donors are less likely to be approached by fundraisers: one study showed that Hispanic donors are highly interested in charitable giving but are less likely than others to be approached by fundraisers; another report indicated one in five African Americans would donate to more organizations if they were asked more often."[3]

Philanthropic communities have not acknowledged this donor base. In Black communities, Greek Life goes beyond college. Starting in the early 1900s, Black sororities and fraternities have been important in providing financial, educational, and other resources for over a hundred years. The Divine Nine[4] (the nine Black Fraternities and Sororities in the US) in the Black community have been instrumental in giving. Unlike most collegiate organizations that end when college is completed, Black Sororities and Fraternities are designed for engagement throughout one's lifetime. These organizations, along with other Black social organizations, like Jack and Jill of America and The Links, Incorporated have provided philanthropy both formally and informally on a local and national level.

Further in the book, details about these organizations and others will demonstrate the lengthy heritage of giving in this country by women and men of color that are making a significant impact in changing the face and narrative of philanthropy. It's important to note that just as poverty exists in all communities, so does wealth. Wealth isn't pervasive in the Black community, but it does exist. This also offers an opportunity for partnership. How can you collaborate with donors of color to make an impact?

Narrative Change: So much of the history of people of color is not included in the textbooks about American history and as a result, many assumptions are made about abilities to contribute to their communities. In the report *Women Give 2019*, the authors state a necessary call to action that nonprofits, foundations, and churches must "expand their donor and volunteer networks by more deeply engaging diverse women and men."[5] As the U.S. population becomes more diverse, embracing these communities can change the trajectory of our communities locally, regionally, and nationally.

Call to Action: On Twitter, there was a trending thread regarding the term, "Black Famous." Names of groups like Maze with Frankie Beverly and other icons in the Black community are not recognized by mainstream radio and television. They were listed to bring awareness to the fact that so much of our culture and history is not included, in not only textbooks but also the awareness or radar of White America. My husband recently told a story that another African American asked him if he was related to Charles Drew because he has the same name. Charles commented that no one White has ever asked him that question but most Black people will ask. Charles Drew was a Black physician who created the technique for blood transfusions. He died because he was unable to receive medical care after a car accident. Many African Americans believed then and now that his death was a result of a White hospital refusing to provide a blood transfusion.[6] Most White Americans have no idea about Charles Drew or other African American scientists, inventors, or those in the history of this country. In this call to action, please take the time to learn more about the Black community and other communities of color. Several of the books on Roy Peter Clark's list entitled "24 books White people should read beyond Black History Month"[7] are some of my favorites. Here are a few to consider:

- *The New Jim Crow: Mass Incarceration in the Age of Color-blindness*, by Michelle Alexander. First came slavery, then came segregation, then came mass incarceration.

- *Between the World and Me*, by Ta-Nehisi Coates. Framed as a letter to his adolescent son, the author digs down to the consequences of the continuing exploitation of Black people in America. The author has made the most eloquent case in favor of reparations for continuing effects of slavery.

- *Beloved*, by Toni Morrison, winner of the Nobel Prize for literature. "Stares unflinchingly into the abyss of slavery." Another must-read is *The Bluest Eye*, a terrifying novel about cultural definitions of beauty and the tragedy of self-hatred.

- *Fences*, by August Wilson. Winner of the Pulitzer Prize for drama, this play depicts what it means for a father to love his son—even at times when he doesn't like him.

- *In Search of Our Mothers' Gardens*, by Alice Walker. Glowing essays expressed in what the author of *The Color Purple* calls "Womanist Prose."

- *Parting the Waters: America in the King Years 1954–63*, by Taylor Branch. Widely hailed by critics of all races as "a vivid tapestry of America."

- *Race Matters*, by Cornel West. From W. E. B. Du Bois to Cornel West, African American intellectuals have helped Americans of all colors understand the sources of racism and the need for change.

- *The Autobiography of an Ex-Colored Man*, by James Weldon Johnson. The 1912 short novel narrates what it means for a person of mixed race to "pass for white" within the system of American apartheid.

- Although I haven't read this, it has been suggested to me many times: *Black and White Styles in Conflict*, by Thomas Kochman. Are Black people and White people the same—or different? Turns out, the answer is "both," according to the White sociologist who drills down into American culture to reveal the sources of our misunderstanding.

- *The Fire Next Time*, by James Baldwin. Framed as a letter to his young nephew on the 100th anniversary of emancipation. A searing call for justice.

- *The Collected Poems of Langston Hughes*. The poet was a Black man in a white world, a gay man in a straight world. His experience of this paradox is important in understanding the many identities that exist within the Black community.

> We are not monolithic and there is tremendous diversity that
> exists within the race. Sadly, if racism was not an issue in the
> Pulitzer Prize judging, he would have won repeatedly.

In reading more about the lives of others, we can better understand their experiences to inform the way we see a difference, and this can direct how our giving can be most impactful. Without a true understanding and clarity of the issues, challenges, and dynamics that exist within the Black Community and other communities of color, there is a disconnect between what is really needed and why. Scripture affirms this in 1 Corinthians 1:10 (KJV): "Now I beseech you, brethren, by the name of our Lord Jesus Christ, that ye all speak the same thing, and that there be no divisions among you; but that ye be perfectly joined together in the same mind and in the same judgment." We can't speak the same thing when we do not understand the struggles and challenges of those around us. Until this is a part of our ethos and way of life, divisions will continue to exist.

10

MYTH: WHITE WEALTH IS NOT BUILT ON SLAVERY

White people must accept that slavery was not a mutually beneficial transaction between Africans and Whites. It was a time in history that Africans were taken from their families, placed in the bottom of ships for over three months with little food, laying in their feces and menstrual blood while only allowed out in the sun periodically to dance for circulation. People were chained to dead bodies without any knowledge of what was happening to them, worried about their families, unaware of where they were being taken to. Once they arrived, they were inspected like animals, placed on auction blocks, and sold to the highest bidder. Women were raped by their slave masters; marriages were not recognized and being beaten or killed was a regular occurrence. They worked mostly on plantations for twelve to sixteen hours a day. Labor in the fields was grueling and those in the house didn't have it easy, either. The fear of being mistreated by the mistress or raped by the master was also a real and regular occurrence. Even after slavery, Black people had to deal with extreme discrimination and racism. Jim Crow laws were created to keep the races separated which lasted until the 1960s. Even with integration in schools and later, the ability to vote, it still did not make up for the wealth, health, and other opportunities that were ignored or denied. While Whites do not want to deal with this travesty of justice, and even though it happened centuries ago, the implications for Blacks are very present today. There is a real danger in the new narrative that Whites are creating about the past to dull its reality and not recognizing how Whites benefit from the past today.

In 2019, Pew Research Center reported the following: "More than eight-in-ten black adults say the legacy of slavery affects the position of black people in America today, including 59% who say it affects it a great deal. About eight in ten blacks (78%) say the country has not gone far enough when it comes to giving black people equal rights with whites, and fully half say it's unlikely that the country will eventually achieve racial equality." The report also stated that almost 60 percent of respondents stated that being White could help one get ahead.[1] There is obviously a disconnect between the way Whites and Blacks experience life in America.

I have heard over and over again by White colleagues that they were not responsible for slavery and that is true. Yet, it is irresponsible not to be aware of the benefit of its legacy for Whites in America. Land and generational wealth have been passed down to White families for generations, one of many factors that contribute to the racial wealth equity gap. According to Dedrick Asante-Muhammad, a coordinator at the Institute for Policy Studies Program on Inequality and the Common Good,

> that includes connections, education and business experience for the descendants of slave owners. It's also specific jobs and industries only open to White workers for decades, as well as contacts and legal protections for white families that never owned slaves. Those benefits were amplified for all white Americans by social practice and policy . . . The jobs most African American and Latino workers held were excluded from the first decades of the Social Security program, while only white Americans were allowed reliable access to the benefits of the GI Bill. From the horrors of the Jim Crow era to school segregation, brutal policing and discrimination in lending, the list goes on.[2]

In the article "Slavery and the Intergenerational Transmission of Human Capital," the author explores the gaps for Blacks in literacy, wages, schooling, and occupations since slavery.[3] The author states: "The past history of slavery undoubtedly shaped institutions and attitudes in the United States." These attitudes have shaped banking/finance, occupational opportunities, and even healthcare. The racial wealth equity gap is a definite remnant from slavery:

> The period that followed the Civil War was one of economic terror and wealth-stripping that has left black people at lasting economic disadvantage. White Americans have seven times the wealth of black Americans on average. Though black people make up nearly 13 percent of the United States population, they hold less than 3 percent of the nation's total wealth. The median family wealth for white people is $171,000, compared with just $17,600 for black people. It is worse on the margins.

According to the Economic Policy Institute, 19 percent of black house-holds have zero or negative net worth. Just 9 percent of white families are that poor.[4]

Redlining, segregation, evictions, and discrimination in banking have con-tributed to the racial wealth equity gap as well.

Eminent domain has also been an issue for Black communities. The "dis-placement of African Americans and urban renewal projects were so inter-twined that urban renewal was referred to as 'Negro removal.'"[5] In many cities across the country, eminent domain has been used to take land from Black homeowners and use it for the benefit of White business owners or the govern-ment. I recently explained to a group why this was and is problematic: Owning land is also having the opportunity to pass it down and when it is taken away, the loss is not just for the immediate family—it is felt for generations.

Racism rears its ugly head in so many areas of our existence. Black and Brown communities also experience environmental injustice as a prolonged effect of slavery. Predominately Black and Brown communities have dealt with issues, such as lead poisoning and illegal dumping, for decades. In West Dallas, Murph Metals began in 1934 smelting lead. The neighborhood com-prised of low-income Black and Brown families experienced lead poison-ing from contamination in the water, air, and soil. According to the *Dallas Morning News*, even decades later the impact of this plant was felt. Several individuals died young, had miscarriages, and experienced various health issues as a result of living in this area: "Figures from the Texas Department of State Health Services show that 31 children age 5 or younger in ZIP code 75212 in West Dallas had blood lead levels of 5 or above . . . And 234 children had levels between 2 and 4, where health effects have been known to occur" in 2012. The full impact isn't known because several did not receive testing and were unaware of the consequences of this hazard.[6]

Another example of environmental injustice is Shingle Mountain in Dal-las. Marsha Jackson purchased the land in the mid-1990s so that her children and grandchildren could ride their horses. Blue Star Recycling purchased land in the area to grind and discard shingles. It grew so large that it was fifty feet away from Marsha's home. Her efforts to get the city of Dallas to do something were futile until articles ran in both the *Dallas Morning News* and *Washington Post*. Jackson now struggles with rashes and coughing up black phlegm. The mountain is "a 60,000–100,000 ton pile of discarded shingles, appropriately called 'shingle mountain,' sits next to her house. Dust from the shingles often blows through the air and into the lungs of Jackson and the rest of the neighborhood's residents." After three years, the City in December

2020 is finally removing the shingles.[7] Imagine if a site like Shingle Mountain existed in more affluent neighborhoods!

Racism for Black people is also evident in medicine. So much of the vaccine hesitancy we are seeing in the Black community stems from a history of inadequate care and downright abuse and mistreatment. Scholar and journalist Linda Villarosa has documented the impact of racism for Blacks in the medical field. She says, "Over the centuries, the two most persistent physiological myths—that black people were impervious to pain and had weak lungs that could be strengthened through hard work—wormed their way into scientific consensus, and they remain rooted in modern-day medical education and practice."[8] In the 1787 manual "A Treatise on Tropical Diseases; and on The Climate of the West-Indies," a British doctor, Benjamin Moseley, claimed that Black people could bear surgical operations much more than White people, noting that "what would be the cause of insupportable pain to a white man, a Negro would almost disregard." To drive home his point, he added, "I have amputated the legs of many Negroes who have held the upper part of the limb themselves."[9] A study was conducted in 2016 to further validate the existence of the belief that Black people are more tolerant to pain:

> This work reveals that a substantial number of white laypeople and medical students and residents hold false beliefs about biological differences between blacks and whites and demonstrates that these beliefs predict racial bias in pain perception and treatment recommendation accuracy. It also provides the first evidence that racial bias in pain perception is associated with racial bias in pain treatment recommendations.[10]

Blacks are often blamed for their unwillingness to seek medical help until it is too late, but it is the historical mistreatment by the medical establishment and racial bias that prevents the care needed for Blacks. In December 2020, Dr. Susan Moore, a physician, died from COVID-19 due to a White doctor who downplayed her symptoms and sent her home, further demonstrating that even with a medical degree, race can be a factor in receiving care.[11] Racial bias, which has been in existence for centuries in the medical field, has real consequences and impact even today.

These issues of the historical implications of slavery influence our perceptions of how wealth was obtained as well. During a meeting at a local foundation, I wanted to tour the grounds of this facility that was once a plantation. On the wall was a framed picture of Africans picking cotton. The employee became visibly concerned because of my presence and told me the family that owned the slaves was very good to them. Although I've never understood the oxymoron of "being good" to someone while holding them without their deserved pay or freedom, this isn't the first time I've heard this comment. Instead of dealing with the guilt, so many create a narrative that sugarcoats the story of those enslaved. There is nothing wrong with wrestling with the truth and understanding the impact of history on present-day realities.

It's a difficult conversation but it is one that must be addressed. The wealth that many acquired in the past was based on the labor of those who were enslaved. If the aforementioned family was truly good to their slaves, it would logically follow that they were paid for their labor and their descendants would benefit from their efforts. Yet, many foundations, universities, and facilities were built by unpaid or low-wage workers.

Colleges like Georgetown have had to deal with this ugly history. In 2017, Georgetown began providing full scholarships to the descendants of the 272 slaves that were sold to pay off its debt in 1838. The University of Virginia established a commission entitled the President's Commission on Slavery and the University to address the university's involvement in slavery including interpretive history on campus, scholarships, and the naming of the buildings after slaves.

This acknowledgment must extend beyond universities and become a serious conversation in the world of foundations, corporate giving, and nonprofits. We must examine this ugly past with more than gestures but with true change and involvement. Representation is not just a picture on a brochure to show diversity but truly creating spaces at the table to share and sometimes cede power. Even in philanthropy, this is something that isn't discussed. So often, Black and Brown bodies that worked to build charitable foundations do not have a voice in the distribution of funding for the communities that are impacted by decisions they did not make or create. It's time for a new narrative that includes the truth of these horrors. A new narrative of philanthropy is needed that adequately addresses the past in order to build a new future.

Narrative Change: We must acknowledge our past and recognize that not everyone has been included. Black people, Latinos, Asians, Native Americans, and the LGBTQ community have been excluded from many tables in the past as well as today. It is important that colleges and other institutions accept and own being on the wrong side of history. I worked on curating the home of Juanita Craft, a civil rights icon locally and nationally. Mrs. Craft, as a Black woman in the 1930s, risked her life setting up NAACP chapters around the state. She taught young people how to organize, using her home as a training ground. Leaders in the Civil Rights Movement came to her home. The State Fair of Texas had one day for Black people called Negro Achievement Day. It was the only day that Black people could enjoy the fair with their families. During Negro Achievement Day, booth owners were allowed to raise their prices. In 1889 "planners first set aside a day for

African Americans to attend the fair. Then called Colored People's Day, it was discontinued in 1910 and renamed Negro Achievement Day in 1936."[12] Mrs. Craft brought a group of Black and White High School students to the Fair with the goal of integrating the event. She was successful! Due to her efforts, the event was integrated in 1961. In her honor, we host an awards program to honor individuals that involved in social justice in the area as well as include her story in the curriculum for schools.[13] The Fair was not previously involved in the local community and, with the creation of my position, I have been able to ensure that we are working with local nonprofits, churches, foundations, and community leaders to do something different through our funding, programming, and connecting the community to resources. The stories are important, and although the State Fair of Texas' history was not inclusive, I am glad to be a part of the team that is changing that narrative.

Call to Action: It's time to own our past and the programming we've received throughout our lives on race, class, gender, and sexuality. As much as people hate being called racist, it is important to know that no matter how many friends you have of another race or even if your children/grandchildren are bi-racial, you can still say and do things that are racist. An article in the *Washington Post* in 2019 addresses this issue: "The threat of appearing racist leads people to overestimate how much their past non-racist actions—like making friends with somebody of another race—are indicative of their non-racist attitudes."[14] Not only is it time that we all become aware but it is time to recognize that even as the most progressive and cool White person in the room, there are still areas that need to be unpacked, addressed, and sometimes it has to happen over and over again. Even as a person of color, I am also learning about the impact of racism on other groups such as the Asian community and the hate they have suffered significantly during COVID-19 or the Latinx community especially around issues of immigration and incarceration. Stop believing that because it did not happen on your watch that it isn't real. It's unfair and arrogant to diminish the experiences of others. How can you begin to unpack some of these beliefs? In the appendix, there is a reading and video list that can help you start. Congratulations on taking the first step. The next step after educating yourself is to begin influencing your network. Creating a book club or a discussion group can be powerful. During my dissertation research, I created a group to study how diverse women build relationships/social capital. I learned a lot from that experience:

1. When people are in safe spaces and have proximity to one another, people will open up and share.

2. Emotions connect us. Even if I don't have the same experience as you do, I can understand loss, hurt, pain, joy, peace,

or fulfillment. We had an individual in the group who experienced extreme abuse at the hands of her mother. None of us could understand the scenario she described but we were heartbroken by imagining the trauma that experience had on her as a child.

3. Perception transformation is real. When we hear stories of others that we are in a relationship with, our perceptions about them and other issues can change. Women in the group had no idea about some of the issues that women of color face as it relates to colorism. That experience was eye-opening and transformative.

4. Cognitive dissonance is important. When it happens, go with the discomfort, and ask yourself why. Cognitive dissonance is "when a person holds two or more contradictory beliefs, ideas, or values, or participates in an action that goes against one of these three, and experiences psychological stress because of it."[15] Wrestle with it instead of ignoring it and continuing life as usual.

One person can make a difference! Are you the person willing and up for the task?

How do these Scriptures inform your thinking and action regarding giving?

God obviously does not see the difference as an issue and recognizes that we all have a purpose regardless of the many groups we may identify with: "For as in one body we have many members, and the members do not all have the same function, so we, though many, are one body in Christ, and individually members one of another." (Romans 12:4-5) (ESV)

We often view unity as making people the same. Understanding is what creates peace, not sameness. "So then let us pursue what makes for peace and for mutual upbuilding." (Romans 14:19) (ESV)

God does not see the differences but recognizes they exist. The many identities we have do not diminish our importance with Christ. "There is neither Jew nor Greek, there is neither slave nor free, there is no male and female, for you are all one in Christ Jesus." (Galatians 3:28) (NIV)

11

MYTH: BIPOCs ARE UNAVAILABLE TO SERVE AND LEAD

The president of Purdue University, Mitch Daniels, commented in 2019 to a group of students of color about Black scholars: "*I will be recruiting one of the rarest creatures in America: a leading, I mean a really leading African American Scholar.*"[1] Daniels did not understand the offense in his comment. First, that Black scholars are creatures was bizarre and unacceptable. There is a long history of Black people being viewed as animals. Secondly, the belief that there are no leading Black scholars is problematic and subjective. There are several African Americans that graduate with PhDs yearly. The online periodical *Journal of Blacks in Higher Education* reports that during the five-year period from 2013 through 2017, 11,389 Black or African American students earned doctoral degrees at colleges and universities in the United States.[2] The heavily populated Facebook page PhinisheD/FinishEdD (Drs/Future Drs) has 15,775 members that are predominantly African Americans with PhDs, EdDs, or in the process of completing their studies toward the terminal degree.

Throughout my career, I have heard the argument that qualified Black people are hard to find whether in academia or nonprofit management. This idea is embedded in our belief system and requires a deeper look into our expectations of BIPOCs versus their White colleagues. There is an unspoken assumption that there is something lacking in candidates of color. I have heard HR managers make statements about "fitting into the culture" which is code for a difference. Subconscious or implicit bias is prevalent in hiring: we typically employ those who are like us. These similarities can be based on race, career history, gender, educational background and more. Implicit Bias, according to the Kirwan Institute at Ohio State University, is

> known as implicit social cognition . . . implicit bias refers to the attitudes or stereotypes that affect our understanding, actions, and decisions in an unconscious manner. These biases, which encompass both favorable and unfavorable assessments, are activated involuntarily and without an individual's awareness or intentional control. Residing deep in the subconscious, these biases are different from known biases that individuals may choose to conceal for the purposes of social and/or political correctness. Rather, implicit biases are not accessible through introspection.[3]

As long as these biases are denied and not addressed, individuals and organizations miss the opportunity to bring in diverse talent that can offer new ideas and accelerate growth.[4] There is a real fear of losing power and change in many organizations. Martin Levine in his *Nonprofit Quarterly* article, "Diversifying Boards Means Ceding Control: Are White Nonprofit Leaders Ready?" challenges power dynamics within white organizations at the board level.[5] Another article, and one that Levine references, is Vanessa Daniels's Op-Ed piece in the New York Times that challenges foundations in their funding. Daniels states, "Only 0.6 percent of foundation giving was targeted to women of color in 2016." Instead of providing funding to women of color-led organizations, which she calls "the bold M.V.P.s of social change," White-led organizations are given opportunities to scale and receive consistent support.[6]

This narrative of nonexistent, not qualified, risky, or lack of capacity in grassroots organizations is not only hindering philanthropy from growth but our communities are suffering because of implicit bias, privilege, and a lack of building bridging social capital. During the first year of the Nonprofit Infrastructure Initiative (a program I built in partnership with the University of North Texas at Dallas and United Way of Dallas), of the ten organizations that pitched for up to ten thousand in funding for their organizations, six requested audits. Smaller organizations cannot bear the financial burden of providing an audit. There are two types of funding in the nonprofit world, restricted and unrestricted. Restricted funds are often grant funds that are designated for a specific project or program. Unrestricted funds are funds that are often from individual donors that do not have stipulations on how funding is used. Without relationships with wealthy donors, many smaller nonprofits do not have access to unrestricted funding that can assist with audits. Foundation funding is restricted, often for programming expenses. There are very few foundations that provide funding for salaries, professional development, legal and accounting services. Many funders do not consider that larger organizations have unrestricted funding to pay for expensive audits and professional development. Most foundations do not cover operating expenses for nonprofits but are more interested in supporting programs. Larger organizations have professional volunteers, that grassroots organizations do not have access to, and those networks that can offset staffing costs. As a donor, consider providing funding to offset the cost of operational expenses such as staffing, utilities, supplies, and training. Tap into your network to volunteer, but check your assumptions at the door. For many of the organizations my department funds, if we only provided financial support for solely programs, many children in the area would not have a meal, a safe place to go after school, or receive enrichment or academic assistance because the staff is necessary for programs to operate.

There is also a belief that there are limited board members of color available to serve on boards. Qualified board members also exist but this depends upon your network and community engagement strategy. If you are unable to find individuals that can serve on boards that are from communities of color, you are not trying. Many corporations have affinity groups that serve marginalized populations. Reaching out to professional organizations like the Society of Professional Hispanic Engineers or the National Association of Black Journalists are resources both nationally and in a number of major cities. As a donor, you have the right to question diverse staffing, board membership, and senior leadership within the organization; and if the numbers are dismal, don't stop there. Tell them it is important to you and begin to build your network in order to help your local organizations and ultimately, your community. Your contributions are votes, and without votes of confidence, accountability, and involvement, things won't change.

Narrative Change: The argument that there are no qualified individuals that are BIPOCs is simplistic and lazy. Highly talented and skilled individuals of all races, backgrounds, and ethnicities obviously exist. It is important to examine your network. If you can't find those individuals, your network is limited and too small. There are so many professional organizations such as the National Society of Black Engineers, Association of Latino Professionals, National Association of Black Accountants, U.S. Hispanic Chamber, and many others that target communities of color. Building partnerships with these groups can help with board membership, targeting individuals for mentors, and other skills that an agency may need. When I was a student at the University of Texas at Arlington, I was a part of a committee that researched trends of hiring faculty of color at the university in the 1990s. At that time, those in leadership would state that they could not find faculty members of color or that they could not pay them comparable salaries because of the demand for their employment. Sadly, the aforementioned quote by the president of Purdue University reaffirms that this thinking still exists. The narrative must change from "they don't exist" to being truthful: we choose not to find them. Donors must hold institutions accountable and ask the hard questions about diversity, inclusion, and equity as it relates to leadership, governance, and funding decisions. We need more organizations to practice inclusive leadership. Inclusive leaders do the following according to an article in *Harvard Business Review*:

Visible Commitment: They articulate authentic commitment to diversity, challenge the status quo, hold others accountable, and make diversity and inclusion a personal priority.

Humility: They are modest about capabilities, admit mistakes, and create the space for others to contribute.

Awareness of Bias: They show awareness of personal blind spots, as well as flaws in the system, and work hard to ensure a meritocracy.

Curiosity about Others: They demonstrate an open mindset and deep curiosity about others, listen without judgment, and seek with empathy to understand those around them.

Cultural Intelligence: They are attentive to others' cultures and adapt as required.

Effective Collaboration: They empower others, pay attention to diversity of thinking and psychological safety, and focus on team cohesion.[7]

Call to Action: There are a number of tools that can be used to address issues of diversity. Using a board matrix is a wonderful tool for nonprofit organizations to use to be strategic regarding board membership. A board matrix lists criteria such as geography, race, age, professional background, and other attributes that are needed in a board member. This type of strategic and intentional thinking must extend not just to the board but to the hiring of staff, volunteers, and even donors to ensure diversity exists. It is not checking off a box. It is recognizing the need for new energy, thinking, and experiences. I sit on a board where I am one of the youngest members and I'm over fifty! That is a problem and I continue to say it. It is important to make sure that we are also bringing younger folks in as well to build a pipeline of leadership. Is this happening in your organization, community, job and if not, what can you do to change it? I would also encourage your organization to consider conducting a racial equity audit.[8]

II

A NEW MODEL TO CHAMPION THE CONTRIBUTIONS OF THOSE BEING SERVED

12

LEVERAGING SOCIAL CAPITAL
FOR CONNECTIONS

S ocial capital is simply defined as the relationships, networks, and associations one has. In the early 1900s, Lyda J. Hanifan, coined the term
to encourage community involvement for student success. Robert
Putnam, the author of *Bowling Alone*, examines social capital in the current context. Putnam analyzed nearly 500,000 interviews with individuals
to determine why social capital has been on the decline in this country. Putnam recognizes that Americans are overwhelmed by their professional and
personal responsibilities and it keeps many of us from connecting with other
people. He says that the challenge America faces is a lack of relationship-
building which is creating a decline in "civic virtue."[1] In 2000, he contended
that lack of social capital results in the decline of civic involvement and
engagement and it is detrimental to the functioning of democracy in the
United States. Putnam built on previous theories to demonstrate that social
capital is vital for societal sustainability. Social capital allows individuals to
build relationships and access to information and resources thus keeping
people engaged and connected.

Putnam demonstrates that social capital has a powerful impact on individuals and communities in the following ways:

- The welfare of children is higher where social capital is higher.
- States where children watch less TV have higher levels of
  social capital
- Murder rates are lower in states where social capital is higher

- People are generally less pugnacious where social capital is higher.

- Where people are connected by dense networks of engagement and reciprocity, they are more likely to comply with the law.

- People that are more connected with each other are also marked by greater tolerance.

- Citizens in high social capital states are likely to do more to reduce inequalities.[2]

Social capital is important because it contributes to community building. Onyx, Edwards, and Bullen's study of seven communities isolated the following areas to determine if they contributed to social capital:

A. Community connections

B. Proactivity/social agency

C. Trust and safety

D. Neighborhood connections

E. Family and friends

F. Tolerance of diversity

G. Value of life

H. Work connections

Trust is the glue and is a vital element of social capital. Relationships are formed through trust. Another study, performed by Zacharakis and Flora, reported that social capital is "based on trust, networks, and shared interests and values."[3] It is clear that social capital is highly beneficial to communities; however, there is less effort to build social capital because of a lack of building connections and trust, leading to more isolation. Because of this, our communities are suffering.

Building social capital in our society is challenging because of the polarization. Gallup's research in February 2020[4] illuminates the issue of isolation due to not finding a prevalence in similar ideological beliefs in a community. We feel as if we are not safe and cannot trust others which keeps us from building community and neighborhood connections.

An essential human process, called bonding, is connecting with other people who are similar to us. Bonding connects groups of individuals together. A study from J. L. Terrion reported that bonding involves connecting to those who are familiar through channels like backgrounds, education levels, and socioeconomic status. Everyone desires to belong and feel a sense of purpose. However, bonding can sometimes limit our ability to tolerate diversity because we are more comfortable with those who are similar to us. It is important to broaden our social capital to interact with people that are different than us.

The real challenge in the growth of our society is to pursue both bonding and bridging social capital. Bridging is connecting with those who are different from us[5] to develop relationships outside of our familiar network. This is important because the information shared in this type of relationship can benefit both heterogeneous and homogeneous communities. In summary, if we remain in similar relationships, we are resharing the same information. Bridging provides an opportunity for new perspectives and new ways of thinking and doing. Issues such as gender, race, class, and poverty can create additional challenges for bonding.[6] If we want to create diverse and inclusive environments, bonding must become a strategy in our personal and professional lives. According to Blokland-Potters and Savage, bridging social capital can simultaneously create bonding social capital when "outsiders" become "insiders." Bridging and bonding social capital become two aspects of one and the same process. How can we think differently about those that are marginalized as outsiders by recognizing the structural and systemic practices that impact their lives? How can we begin to examine our networks as opportunities to bridge with those who are different with the goal of creating bonding social capital organically?

There is a benefit in building social capital, not only for our neighborhoods but for our health. Social capital can be "associated with good health, good educational outcomes, lower crime, and a stronger community."[7] When we are intentional about building relationships, it can transform our lives. The Gospel of Mark states, "The second is this: 'You shall love your neighbor as yourself.' There is no other commandment greater than these" (Mark 12:31 NIV). When we think of our neighbors, we are often thinking about those who live in close proximity but neighbors are not only referring to where we live. It is about making an effort to build relationships with those who might have different views, backgrounds, or ways of life. I want the best for my daughter. However, as a Christian, it is my duty to want that for all people and not just for those who are like me. When we work together, we will see changes in our communities that can impact crime, education, and overall well-being, but it starts with acknowledging the past, recognizing the impact on the present, and re-imaging the future in partnership and not paternalism.

As those who give and fund organizations or programs, we can no longer view those who we financially support as outsiders. They must inform our decisions in giving. We can no longer be passive in our relationships with nonprofits when it relates to our giving and volunteering. We need to develop relationships with those we serve, ask the hard questions of these organizations, and begin to find opportunities that we can engage at a deeper level to ensure that we are really connecting to those communities rather than just writing a check. A friend of mine is the founder of a nonprofit organization. On a site visit, a funder came to see the home for teen mothers and inappropriately interrogated the young women about their families and decisions. Our job as funders is not to demean or belittle those who are being served. It's our job to understand not only the organizations we are funding but the context in which those organizations exist along with the cultural and historical dynamics that particularly impact the community being served. Asking questions about the community, the clients served, what success looks like for the agency and for those they serve are important. Connecting with the Executive Director, Board Chair, or even the Program Director can offer insight into the organization. Review websites, social media, and annual reports but realize the smaller, grassroots nonprofits may not have these or have the time to consistently update. This can become a real opportunity to partner in these areas.

As a funder, relationships with our partners are key to our work. When I started at the State Fair of Texas, we were experiencing an onslaught of media attention. I was hired as Director of Community Affairs to provide funding from revenue generated by the event to local organizations as well as support community initiatives. Although I had been in the area for years because of my work at St. Philip's, the African American Museum, the South Dallas Cultural Center as well as my church, Cornerstone Baptist, I could not assume that I understood the area. I spent months listening. I remember one community leader I have known for years went off on me. I asked her later why she did that and she responded that she never had an opportunity to share her thoughts. So often in communities, we do not create the space for people to share the totality of their feelings and experiences. We assume we know what is best for them and instead of taking the time to build trust, we immediately assume we know what's best for them and that's not only arrogant, but it's also irresponsible. All of the programs I created had nothing to do with what I thought would be best. I listened to the community first, built relationships, and leveraged existing ones before creating any program or spending any money. Take the time to listen and learn first. Do not take the responses personally. As I realized, the problems were much bigger than me. It was about a history that was never addressed and a space that had never been created. Listening leads to opportunities for reconciliation.

Creating space for relationship building is necessary even when we do not understand the differences involved. As much as money can make a difference in a community, relationships are even more powerful. In addition to building relationships with those in a local area, how can you leverage your existing network to bring resources? In every role I have had in the last twenty years, I consistently brought a network with me to help solve issues. It first requires listening to the needs of the area, identifying existing untapped resources in the area, and then leveraging your social capital to bring others in to serve.

Narrative Change: I have discovered that Black, Brown, and other communities of color know what they need. They often do not have access to the resources to make these changes. We must change the narrative of coming into communities to solve issues on behalf of others and instead stand in solidarity with those there and doing work on the ground. It starts with moving from a missionary mindset to a mindset of one who is there to support. In Luke 10:25-37, Jesus provides an illustration that is helpful in our current context. The Samaritan in those days was an outsider to the Jewish community. There was a man who was beaten by robbers, something beyond his control that impacted his mobility, his health, and his resources. The religious figures, the priest and Levite, moved to the other side and chose not to get involved even though their belief system commands assisting others in need. They allowed their attitudes to keep them from truly embracing what they said they believed. It was a Samaritan man who was the one who stopped. Samaritans and Jews hated one another and yet, he did not allow political or cultural differences to impact his decision to get involved. When he encountered the man, he did not chastise him about his decisions. He didn't ask what happened; he saw the need and began to address it. He got involved, gave his time and resources by using oil, cared for the Samaritan man's wounds, and obtained a place for him to stay. He even used his network, the innkeeper, to assist until he returned. He did not do something wonderful, applaud his efforts, and walk away. He was committed and planned to return. Jesus commands us to do likewise. Our role is not to separate ourselves. It is to be in the community. We are to be available, listen, and support where and when needed.

Call to Action: I visited a physical therapist after a car accident, and he spoke words that have resonated with me decades later: He said we are human *beings* and not human *doings*. I find that so often in our desire to make a difference and help others, we want to do something immediately. A White friend saw a video of me talking about race for our ABC local network and wanted to do something. She was stunned when my response was "not now." I asked her to instead listen first. I told her to co-create the space to share, build relationships and then collaboratively do something in partnership. How can you create spaces in your community to listen even when the content may be painful? How can you implement critical reflection in those moments of listening?

Reflect on previous interactions in the past in marginalized communities. What can you do differently? "Reflecting in action" is to think about the situation as it is occurring. Instead of being so quick to respond or offer solutions, how can you be present in the moment to listen, ask questions, ask for clarity, and seek understanding? Reflecting for action is another component of critical reflection.[8] Instead of making decisions immediately, how can you think about what you've learned or the interaction?

Reflecting is important but it is also critical to see things from a view different than your own. Reframing is important. Reframing is "a different way of looking at a situation, person, or relationship by changing its meaning."[9] How can you see the situation from not only your perspective but from the perspective of others, recognizing that their lived experiences are different and that they will see things differently? How can you adjust your thinking as needed based on what you have learned and your reflection?[10]

Scriptures to Ponder

Spend some time meditating on these Scriptures and how they relate to building relationships:

Hebrews 10:24 (KJV): "And let us consider one another to provoke unto love and to good works."

Proverbs 18:2 (ESV): "A fool takes no pleasure in understanding, but only in expressing his opinion."

Titus 3:2 (ESV): "To speak evil of no one, to avoid quarreling, to be gentle, and to show perfect courtesy toward all people."

13

FLOURISHING AND THE INCREASE
OF OTHER FORMS OF CAPITAL

Working in South Dallas has made me keenly aware of the assets in marginalized communities that exist are often overlooked. It's so easy to see blight without realizing the wealth that exists. Dr. Tara J. Yosso coined the Community Cultural Wealth model, which elaborates on the assets that young people from low-income communities have as first-generation college students. The sociologist Pierre Bourdieu is responsible for creating the term "cultural capital" which serves as a foundation for Yosso's work. Cultural capital is the way in which a person uses their education, knowledge, speech, and dress to move through society. Having these attributes can help one move through society building their social status and power. Just as those assets are embodied in young people, they are also embedded in the communities they are from. In my work in South Dallas, I see these assets daily at work. Yosso's model demonstrates that we cannot take for granted the assets and cultural capital that exists within individuals and communities, no matter where they are from or live.

According to Yosso, there are six forms of capital: aspirational, linguistic, familial, social, navigational, and resistance. Aspirational capital is the "ability to maintain hope and dreams for the future in the face of real and perceived barriers."[1] In South Dallas, I have witnessed young people who have been a part of our NXT Fest planning committee develop a college and career fair for more than four hundred students. As they are planning for college, while finishing high school, these young people face tremendous odds. It is an area that is isolated from many of the amenities such as restaurants, banks, and retail shopping that exist in suburbs. Several highways divide the area from many needed resources. "The creation of I-30 and I-45 destabilized the area greatly. I-45 cut the eleven-square-mile neighborhood in half, I-30 disconnected it from the job base, and the Trinity River Forest's boundaries separated it from the rest of the region."[2] The population has not grown much in twenty years. It is a community of less than twelve thousand that lacks employment opportunities and grocery stores, and has limited new housing. In South Dallas, "the average household earns $42,000, with 60 percent earning less than $35,000 and the average in Dallas-Fort Worth metroplex is $96,000."[3] Yet despite these odds, several of the young people from this neighborhood attend college, like Alisa who graduated from Lincoln High school and recently received her PhD. The aspirational capital also exists in the nonprofits and community leaders in the area. Pastor Chris Simmons of Cornerstone Baptist Church shares that he when arrived as a graduate student in the late 1980s to pastor the church, it was a war zone. Drugs and criminal activity were rampant in the area. Pastor Chris asked the congregation: if they left, would it matter to the community? He decided to stay because he believed in this community and its residents and he was able to play a huge part in the transformation of this area. Pastor Chris partners with many churches in North Dallas that are well-resourced to leverage both financial and social capital to build this community. Cornerstone provides several free programs to the residents in the community, including afterschool programs, summer day camps, a medical clinic, a dental clinic, a community garden, transitional housing programs, meals for those in need, a clothing closet, and the Christmas store. Even during the COVID-19 pandemic, the church has remained a lifeline for the community by offering free meals and a laundromat for the homeless to wash clothing. One day, while feeding the hundreds of homeless, a man asked to take a shower. Pastor Chris felt it was not safe because the pandemic had just started. The man told him that it had been weeks since he was able to do so. Pastor Chris realized his privilege. We could shower and had access to hygiene products. They did not. Using faith, love, and hope, Pastor Chris Simmons opened the shower and created measures to make sure it was both accessible and safe for a population that had been largely forgotten during the pandemic.

The second form of capital Yosso references is linguistic. Linguistic capital is the ability to communicate using the lived experiences or stories. Many young people serve as translators for their family members who speak Spanish or have poor literacy skills. "According to the U.S. Department of Education, 54% of U.S. adults 16-74 years old—about 130 million people—lack proficiency in reading, reading below the equivalent of a sixth-grade level."[4] In the communities in South Dallas, literacy is an issue. I visited the Literacy Instruction for Texas (LIFT) in the area a few years ago. I was shocked to see the class was comprised of Black senior citizens who were learning to read. These individuals had raised families, had grandchildren, and many were reading on an elementary level. Many of our young people are paying bills and resolving legal issues because of the literacy levels of their parents and grandparents. Years ago when I worked at World Vision as National Director of Community Engagement, I visited Belzoni, Mississippi, in the Delta, one of the poorest areas in the United States. While touring the K–12 complex, many desks were empty. I remember asking one of the administrators where all the students were. I was told that because it was the first of the month, many of the kids were helping their parents pay bills.

Not only is literacy a challenge but we often miss out on the lived experiences and stories that create these challenges in communities when we do not listen. Our narratives are important and share so much about our identities. When we do not create spaces to listen and see the stories as critical to understanding a community or even rebuilding it, we are destined to make mistakes because we are missing out on critical information. Just as individuals have stories, so do our communities. Being open to listening to those stories is important. I learned so much just by asking questions without judgment. Stories are an asset in communities.

There are so many lessons in the story of Nehemiah. Nehemiah sat down and wept before God because Jerusalem was in ruins after the Babylonian exile (Nehemiah 1:4). He sought God. As a society, we need moments to lament and mourn over the damage that has been done within our communities. We also need to recognize our knowledge is limited and there are issues that are chronic in our communities. We cannot do this alone. We need God to guide and lead us in changing our hearts, in changing the way we see ourselves and others so that we can better understand God's will for ALL of our lives. In the book of Nehemiah, rebuilding the walls was important because if the city is not well, safe, and protected, the places of worship would also be impacted and left exposed. Nehemiah used his position in the king's court to seek permission to make a difference. We must take a look at our power and privilege and use them for the betterment of others. Nehemiah 5 demonstrates that even in this fragile state, there was still exploitation of those who were needy. Nehemiah calls us to care for those who are struggling. He calls for reconciliation and restoration. Yet he didn't just call for caring for the poor, he used his own resources to help. In addition, he tapped into the talents of those around him to assist. Nehemiah focused on repairing something that he didn't destroy. He knew that the wall wasn't just about keeping people out as much as it was about protecting those within who were vulnerable and being mistreated. It's important that we realize our responsibility in rebuilding what we may not have destroyed but we know will benefit others.

Rebuilding a community starts with recognizing the importance of relationships and the role of the family. When families are struggling, our cities are vulnerable and exposed. Families are important in communities. Strong families are the fabric for strong communities. Families are diverse—they range from nuclear families to grandparents raising grandchildren. When I was growing up, I had individuals that I called my uncle or aunt who were not biologically related to me but served in that honorary role. Traditionally, this is not unusual in Black families. When we think of Black families, we often see brokenness and disruption, and this is not true. The reality is that "family" does not just consist of immediate household members but comprises extended family members, friends, church members, and neighbors. A close friend and I met when she moved to South Dallas in the late 1990s. She was a single mother of four, escaping a marriage of drug usage and domestic violence. For her children, I was their aunt because of my presence in their lives. They are all adults now and still call me "Aunt Froswa." Families come in so many forms and the power of familial capital cannot be dismissed in challenged communities. When we tap into the knowledge and lived experience of these relationships, it is a crucial resource. There is a wealth of wisdom and context that is valuable for transforming communities.

Being poor does not mean you do not have relationships. Yosso challenges us to remove the belief that BIPOCs "'lack' the social and cultural capital required for social mobility."[5] Social capital, which was discussed in the previous chapter, is also important to note. It is sometimes assumed the communities that have been neglected do not have access to social networks. This is not accurate. Silvia Dominguez and Celeste Watkins wrote an article entitled "Creating Networks for Survival and Mobility: Social Capital among African-American and Latin-American Low-Income Mothers." They noted that low-income mothers have a social network of daycare providers that include relatives, neighbors, friends, and institutions. Because many of these women are low-wage earners, they do not have sick days. If they take off, they do not get paid, unlike salaried positions. If their kids are sick or there is bad weather, they cannot afford to stay home. It is through informal networks that they can care for their children and survive. "Social capital that improves opportunities for upward mobility can be obtained from relationships that provide advice, contacts, and encouragement to get ahead."[6] Networks are critical for individual and community success. What does it look like when we tap into the networks of low-income communities along with those of more resourced areas to create change? The possibilities are endless.

When I am teaching community development practices, I often ask participants how many systems people encounter in poor neighborhoods. I'll list a few: educational, healthcare (clinics, public hospitals), employment (unemployment office), benefits (TANF, Social Security, WIC), food (grocery stores, pantries, convenience stores), transportation (public, shared), criminal justice (police, constables, sheriffs, peace officers, highway patrol, judges, courts, jails/prisons)—and this isn't comprehensive. It is overwhelming and the ability to navigate through these different policies, rules, and regulations requires a lot of information and stamina. Many of us do not even comprehend this or have limited, if any, interactions with most listed. Dealing with these systems requires navigating bureaucracy to get one's needs met. It's challenging when a person is trying to receive help only to be rerouted repeatedly leading to discouragement or the issue resulting in some type of negative action because help was not found soon enough.

Yosso's work primarily focuses on young people. Just as young people must navigate so many realities in under-resourced communities such as help for college, finding jobs, or even internet access for school, it is indeed a part of the daily life of most. Navigational capital is maneuvering spaces and institutions that are hostile or unsupportive. Years ago, when working at St. Philip's, I knew of a family with seven children. The parents worked so hard to care for their children, but during the month of December, their electricity was cut off. They could not afford the fees to turn it back on nor pay the bill. A dear friend of mine worked for a local bank, and I told her about the situation. She called a former assistant police chief who made a call to get it back on. This family called the same number repeatedly to find help only to hear automated messages. This story illustrates the power of relationships. Notice the difference. When the family called, they did not receive help. When a person utilized their network, things happened. This situation demonstrates not only the power of social networks but the challenges that individuals have when they do not have a network or the knowledge to navigate how to get their needs met. Navigational capital is a valuable skill that is necessary for survival.

Yosso also describes the fight that BIPOCs have endured. Resistance capital is the ability to deal with oppression and fight for equity and equality. Fighting for social justice creates the ability to not only recognize problems but visualize possibilities for solving them. There is a legacy of overcoming that is a crucial part of our communities. South Dallas has experienced so much neglect and a lack of investment and yet, this community and others like it, continue to see leaders rise up to speak out and demand change. Leaders like former councilwoman, Diane Ragsdale, have been instrumental in change, such as developing affordable housing and retail in the area through her nonprofit, Innercity Development Corporation (ICDC). She continues to mentor other leaders and offers her expertise to initiatives like the South Dallas/Fair Park Transportation Initiative to create more options for residents to have access to public transportation. There are so many others that I do not have space to recognize them and their contributions but know that they exist.

Why is it important to be aware of this? When individuals come to serve in urban areas, they assume the people in the communities have nothing to offer, so they bring resources. Most do not see the assets that exist within the communities, the people, and their institutions. In addition to not understanding the historical context, they focus only on the lack and not the power that is already there. What happens when these assets are leveraged within these communities and outside resources are then available to stand in the gap in coordination with those communities? The result is not a community that is surviving but one that thrives because these resources are identified, acknowledged, and given the opportunity to flourish.

Narrative Change: My daughter is a college student, and one of the things I often challenge her about is this idea of "either/or." It is so easy to pick one because it makes it easy for us, but it leaves out so many possibilities. I often challenge her to see the multiple realities, or the "both/and," that exist in each situation. In our communities, there are multiple realities that exist at the same time. In under-resourced areas, there is a lack of resources and yet, there are untapped resources that exist within the individuals in those communities. We must be willing to change the narrative from viewing these areas and their residents as destitute to viewing the areas that are filled with possibilities because we now are aware of the multiple assets that exist in the people.

Call to Action: In the next chapter, Asset Mapping will be discussed. Recognizing the assets within individuals and within communities is critical. Yosso's model of cultural wealth changes our view of individuals from low-income communities from lacking to recognizing the power that exists. Can you think of examples of how this shows up in your local community? As your organization, church, or program decides to volunteer in communities, how can you identify these forms of cultural capital first in order to view the community from a different lens?

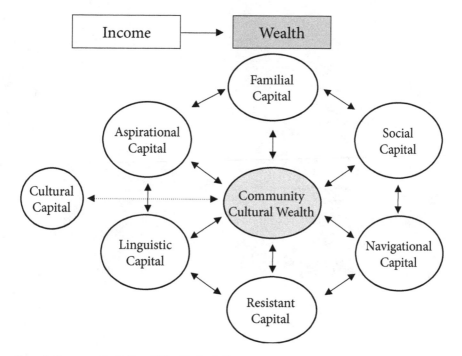

Yosso's Community Cultural Wealth Model[7]

14

KNOWING YOUR COMMUNITY
AND ASSET MAPPING

As mentioned in the previous chapter, we often do not acknowledge the assets that exist within under-resourced communities. In South Dallas, people are unaware of theater companies, like Soul Rep Theater Company or dance companies, such as TMJ Dance Project. They are unaware of the South Dallas Cultural Center which features performances, classes, and art exhibits. They do not know about great schools, like St. Philip's, St. Anthony's, or Dunbar Elementary. They don't know about restaurants that have some of the most delicious food, like Two Podners' or Blackjack Pizza. They don't know about civil rights icon Juanita Craft, who was responsible for integrating the State Fair of Texas, and her home on Warren Avenue; or the house museum of Kathlyn Gilliam, the first Black female school board member in Dallas. This list goes on and on of hidden gems in this area and to those from the outside, they see South Dallas as a place that is lacking. Yes, there are severe needs and yet, there are institutions, associations, and businesses that are a part of this community. Knowing these assets can make a difference in the way we view and interact with these communities.

During my days at World Vision, I witnessed this as I traveled to our sites in US Programs across the country. Some places—like Albany, Georgia or Immokalee, Florida or the Bronx in New York City, Compton in Los Angeles, California, or Phillipa, West Virginia—have struggled with issues similar to South Dallas, such as affordable housing, education, drug usage, or limited employment opportunities. In my work, I realized very quickly that despite the similarities, there was a real difference being made in each of these areas. Once, I was arguing with a cab driver who would not take me to the World Vision facility in West Chicago because he said the area was too dangerous. Eventually, he gave in and realized that I was not a bad person nor was the area. This happens all around our country. We stereotype areas and deny resources to thousands because of the actions of a few. Note that crime still occurs in affluent neighborhoods and it doesn't change the access those residents have to resources. Pizza companies and food delivery companies will not deliver in South Dallas except to Fair Park. Otherwise, community members must drive out of the neighborhood to enjoy variety. Stereotypes tend to plague communities especially because of the media and perception. Our local newspaper reported one day that there was a killing near my job in Fair Park, yet the incident happened in a completely different area miles away. Using the location of the Park was not only inaccurate, but it fed into the stereotypes about the neighborhood. When all we hear and see on television are negative images and reports, we are fearful to engage in these areas. These reports very seldom highlight the assets in these communities made up of everyday people who desire a better life for themselves and their families. These stereotypes ultimately impact our interactions. According to scholar Carolyn West, "Some stereotypes have been activated so frequently, for example through media exposure, that these representations can occur non-consciously in the mere presence of a stereotyped group member. If an individual chooses to accept a stereotype, or if he or she simply does not think about it, then the image can influence the way in which they perceive and interact . . ."[1] Mere perceptions can cause so much damage and dims our ability to see people the way God sees each of us. This deprives individuals and communities of relationships and opportunities through partnerships.

When we fail to recognize the assets (including people) in an area, our lens is clouded, and we cannot accurately view what exists or the potential and possibilities for collaboration. Working in communities that are under-resourced requires the *identification of internal assets first before bringing in outside resources to create change. External resources cannot dictate the change in an area but should only serve as a partner in the transformation.*

A wonderful tool that I have used for decades to do this work is Asset-Based Community Development (ABCD) which is a theory developed by two scholars, Jody Kretzman and John McKnight of DePaul University. ABCD does not look at the deficits that exist in a community but focuses on the assets. McKnight and Kretzmann (1993) found that among all the assets that exist in the community, ABCD enables "individuals to pay particular attention to the assets inherent in social relationships as evident in formal and informal associations and networks."[2] All the assets that exist within a community are held together by social relationships. ABCD encourages communities to identify assets through five categories (associations, institutions, public space, local economy, and individuals—more recent documents include a sixth category, stories). The work of Kretzmann and McKnight provide communities an opportunity to first identify what exists, tap into those resources, and build relationships beyond their area based on an understanding of what is needed to create the necessary change identified by citizens.

When I started at the State Fair of Texas, using this lens was critical for the work. Without understanding what existed in South Dallas, it was easy to duplicate efforts and create distrust amongst our organization and community stakeholders. Asset mapping is not easy. It requires the ability to have relationships in the community because you will not be able to know everything that exists on your own. Yet, using this lens changed the way I saw communities in my work at World Vision, around the country, and in South Dallas at the State Fair. It also changed the way we have funded organizations. We focus on small to mid-sized nonprofits because our community has so many that are under the radar by major foundations but are providing critical assistance. Even in my role at HERitage Giving Circle, our focus has been on small, Black female-led organizations. Yet, without relationships in the community, we would not have known how to contact these organizations. Data has shown that only six-tenths of a percent of all funding in this country supports organizations led by Black women in 2016.[3] These organizations are doing the work but often aren't at tables to make decisions or speak about their work. I often hear that people cannot find individuals or organizations. Much of this is due to their own discomfort to ask and unwillingness to partner.

Asset mapping can help with identifying these organizations, potential programming opportunities, funding, and volunteers. Sororities and Fraternities are different in the Black community. Membership is for a lifetime[4] because those who are active remain involved beyond college through graduate chapters. In my organization, Alpha Kappa Alpha, Sorority, Inc., members are still included even in death as an Ivy Beyond the Wall. There are nine recognized Greek organizations in the Black community and all are committed to service. As you are partnering in Black or Brown communities, how can you identify groups like this and other associations for projects? I've seen well-meaning organizations donate funds and items to organizations because they saw them on a website without having knowledge or relationship to determine if the organization is really connected to the communities they claim to serve. How can your organization work with local schools and colleges to create asset maps that can be a resource for the entire community? Before moving forward, determine if what you are doing already exists.

We noticed at the State Fair of Texas that many of the organizations in the Southern Sector of Dallas did not have the platform they needed to share their story. Storytelling is so important. In partnership with Julie Morris and Persona Media Co., we created ServeSouthernDallas.org during COVID-19 as a way to amplify the voices of these leaders and their organizations. The State Fair, prior to this website, created a resource guide for our community as well as an app called Community Connections for our local area to have as another resource. We realized that we didn't know everyone in the neighborhood (and we still don't!) but this not only helps us but our neighbors as well. We update this resource quarterly to make sure it is current. During COVID-19, I started calls with our agencies so that they could coordinate services and support one another. Things as simple as creating spaces for convening can make a difference in building community between residents or community organizations. Imagine bringing these groups together from across the city or region to share? It's a great way to build community, create the space for sharing, and open the door to collaboration.

Narrative Change: No matter the challenges a community faces, there are multiple assets that exist within the residents and in the area. As philanthropists, volunteers, or just concerned individuals, we must question our stereotypes and thinking regarding under-resourced communities. It is not only a disservice to these areas, but it limits our ability to build relationships when we see these communities as less than, especially when we fail to recognize the impact of media, history, and bias. The narrative must become one that not only changes our thinking but the way we act toward and support these areas with our resources.

Call to Action: Asset Mapping serves a dual purpose. It allows one to identify what exists within your community but also the resources that exist within your organization. In Exodus 4:2, God asks Moses, "What is that in your hand?" So often we are seeking resources outside of ourselves instead of knowing what already have at our disposal. Moses' staff was capable of doing what he needed. The same principle applies when we begin to think of what we have available based on our heart, our head, and our hands. Before starting something new, focus on what are you passionate about. What do you have available in terms of physical and mental resources? What are your skills? If you are a part of an organization, what does this look like as well? What are your "Ps": physical resources (clothing, products), people resources, and plant resources (facility/land)? How can these be used to make a difference? Knowing our assets as well as the assets in a community are a great way to begin an inventory of what exists. As I work with

Fairs across the country to think about their assets, I often challenge them to think about their property/land as an opportunity to engage community members. How could you allow space for programming? Could you work with your local hospital to have a mammogram unit provide free to low-cost services, coordinate with your transportation provider rides for participants, and offer a meal and daycare for those who attend? Could you work with a local organization in an under-resourced community to bring this resource to them? Using an asset map as a tool can help you think strategically about addressing needs in your area through relationships and partners.

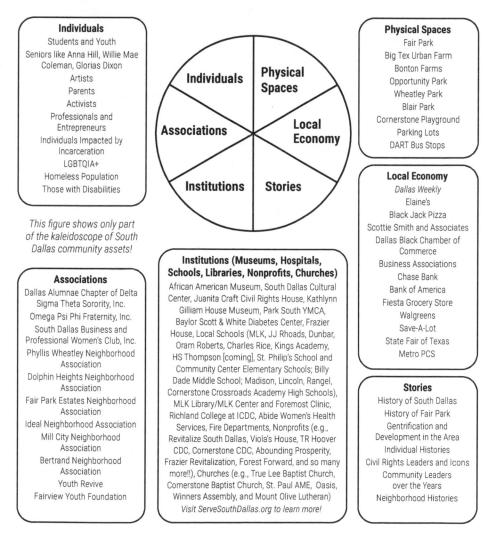

Individuals
Students and Youth
Seniors like Anna Hill, Willie Mae Coleman, Glorias Dixon
Artists
Parents
Activists
Professionals and Entrepreneurs
Individuals Impacted by Incarceration
LGBTQIA+
Homeless Population
Those with Disabilities

This figure shows only part of the kaleidoscope of South Dallas community assets!

Associations
Dallas Alumnae Chapter of Delta Sigma Theta Sorority, Inc.
Omega Psi Phi Fraternity, Inc.
South Dallas Business and Professional Women's Club, Inc.
Phyllis Wheatley Neighborhood Association
Dolphin Heights Neighborhood Association
Fair Park Estates Neighborhood Association
Ideal Neighborhood Association
Mill City Neighborhood Association
Bertrand Neighborhood Association
Youth Revive
Fairview Youth Foundation

Physical Spaces
Fair Park
Big Tex Urban Farm
Bonton Farms
Opportunity Park
Wheatley Park
Blair Park
Cornerstone Playground
Parking Lots
DART Bus Stops

Local Economy
Dallas Weekly
Elaine's
Black Jack Pizza
Scottie Smith and Associates
Dallas Black Chamber of Commerce
Business Associations
Chase Bank
Bank of America
Fiesta Grocery Store
Walgreens
Save-A-Lot
State Fair of Texas
Metro PCS

Institutions (Museums, Hospitals, Schools, Libraries, Nonprofits, Churches)
African American Museum, South Dallas Cultural Center, Juanita Craft Civil Rights House, Kathlynn Gilliam House Museum, Park South YMCA, Baylor Scott & White Diabetes Center, Frazier House, Local Schools (MLK, JJ Rhoads, Dunbar, Oram Roberts, Charles Rice, Kings Academy, HS Thompson [coming], St. Philip's School and Community Center Elementary Schools; Billy Dade Middle School; Madison, Lincoln, Rangel, Cornerstone Crossroads Academy High Schools), MLK Library/MLK Center and Foremost Clinic, Richland College at ICDC, Abide Women's Health Services, Fire Departments, Nonprofits (e.g., Revitalize South Dallas, Viola's House, TR Hoover CDC, Cornerstone CDC, Abounding Prosperity, Frazier Revitalization, Forest Forward, and so many more!!), Churches (e.g., True Lee Baptist Church, Cornerstone Baptist Church, St. Paul AME, Oasis, Winners Assembly, and Mount Olive Lutheran)
Visit ServeSouthDallas.org to learn more!

Stories
History of South Dallas
History of Fair Park
Gentrification and Development in the Area
Individual Histories
Civil Rights Leaders and Icons
Community Leaders over the Years
Neighborhood Histories

South Dallas Community Asset Map (Partial)[5]

15

WEAVING NETWORKS ACTUALLY WORKS

One of the most rewarding experiences of my career was meeting June Holley, the author of the *Network Weaver Handbook*. I met June through a platform created by Spark Collaboration that connects individuals within organizations and companies. June was someone that I have admired for her work in bringing together groups to make a difference. I was fortunate to bring her to Dallas to work with nonprofits through our Community Engagement Day with the University of North Texas at Dallas. After that time, I had the pleasure of working with her and the prize fellows of Robert Wood Johnson Foundation to train their team on networking principles. She's a gifted human being with such skill, insight, and wisdom. Her experience in network weaving is unparalleled.

Networking Weaving is more than just social capital. It is important to build relationships and have networks, but it's something altogether different when you can mobilize networks into action. "A Network Weaver is aware of the networks around them and explicitly works to make them healthier (more inclusive, bridging divides). Network Weavers do this by connecting people strategically where there's potential for mutual benefit, helping people identify their passions, and serving as a catalyst for self-organizing groups."[1] I use networking weaving when I host events like Community Engagement Day or my monthly calls with nonprofits to help them think about the ways in which they can strategically connect to one another.

Building social capital is important, but if we do not take it a step further into using that capital to make a difference; then, we have relationships that may benefit us but not the greater good. According to *A Network Approach to Capacity Building*, "A networked group of people and/or organizations can act in concert to accomplish what cannot be accomplished individually by building relationships for sharing knowledge, goods and experiences and . . . learning from each other."[2]

As a donor, one of the most impactful things that you can do in addition to writing a check is introducing your network to those organizations that you are supporting. Networks create opportunities for innovation and creativity because of the sharing of ideas and resources.

There are four different roles that exist in a network: connector, project coordinator, facilitator, and guardian. A connector is someone who sees the gaps and identifies relationships to solve the issue. For example, when I worked at St. Philip's, I noticed that many of our young people were not exposed to non-traditional sports. Most aspired to play basketball or football as an opportunity to leave poverty. Yet, the percentage of young people who are recruited to those leagues is in the hundreds compared to the tens of thousands of high school players who dream of being a part of the NBA or the NFL. Instead, I reached out to the National Lacrosse League to inquire about possibilities to bring a team to our community. They connected me with Edie Lycke who was been a fierce champion of the sport. She was the founder of Bridge Lacrosse and because of her passion, the program brought together young people from the more affluent North Dallas schools to South Dallas to teach students how to play. We started a girls' and boys' team which almost twenty years later, still exists. This program opened doors for several of our students to attend prominent private schools that had lacrosse leagues but provided an opportunity for college scholarships. This program was about more than opening doors for our students. It also created relationships between the students from the North Dallas schools to have experiences in our community that changed their perspectives about the people and the place. In addition to this nontraditional sport, I also had the opportunity to bring fencing classes to our youth, again, with the goal of exposure and increased opportunities. In this role, I served as a Connector. I saw a challenge and I brought individuals together to address it. Connectors see opportunities to bring resources through their network to make a difference.

Project Coordinators also play an important role in a network. A Project Coordinator is the one who often leads and organizes the people and the tasks in a network. They manage the network. Our work with the Nonprofit Infrastructure Initiative with United Way and the State Fair of Texas required significant coordination. United Way served in the project coordinator role by not only creating the applications for the cohort and organizing the interviews for the agencies that were finalists for participation, but once the cohort was in full swing, they also sent invitations to the group and coordinated the sessions in collaboration with the State Fair of Texas. Each cohort was able to fully engage because of the administrative support that was provided to address any potential issues. We have been fortunate to have several individuals who helped make this a success over the four years of the cohort—Paola Martinez, Aisha Luck, and Nissy New have been gems for their coordination expertise. It has been because of our partnership that they were able to make sure that each cohort was organized and successful. Networks can happen unexpectedly but for them to be successful, there must be coordination. In communities, a coordinator is not always in place at the start of a network, but as it grows there will be the need for this role.

Depending on the situation, I tend to serve in a variety of roles as a Network Weaver. When COVID-19 became a real issue in our area, many of our nonprofits in the South Dallas area were on the front lines providing services. I remember several needed help identifying products to distribute. For many of us, we were unaware that diapers and wipes were limited. This not only was an issue in low-income areas but individuals with resources could not find them in the stores, either. World Vision[3] has a wonderful warehouse in our area and has products that nonprofit members can tap into. In many communities, nonprofits can access donated products or partner with organizations like Good360.org that provide an array of products like building supplies, toys, and clothing. So often when nonprofits are seeking funding, I can go through their budget to find ways to offset many costs of items with donated products. Because of the sense of urgency we were experiencing during COVID-19, not only were products a necessity for those in need, but it was also important to coordinate with our agencies to eliminate the duplication of services and to have more efficient operations for the community. I started bringing our agencies together to meet weekly to discuss their involvement as well as their needs. The initial fifteen agencies have grown to more than double in attendance. We have expanded it from those in our immediate area to those in surrounding neighborhoods. It has increased partnerships and collaboration in programming. This is an example of network facilitation. This is bringing a group of individuals together to address an issue or solve for one. A Network Facilitator serves an important role as a convener.

A Network Guardian is another important role in a network. This is an individual or group interested in the well-being of the network. This can be expressed in several ways. The South Dallas Employment Project is one example of a Network Guardian relationship. We have more than eighty organizations that are involved to provide those impacted by incarceration employment, national-level certifications, and support resources like housing, advocacy, transportation, and mental health services. In addition to bringing these organizations together to coordinate their services, the network provides information and resources to the member organizations to build their capacity. In addition to being a managing partner of this project with Redemption Bridge, a local nonprofit, we support our nonprofits through training and education. Another example of network guardianship was during the early stages of the COVID-19 virus spread, we wanted to highlight organizations that are led by Black and Brown leaders of nonprofits in the Southern Sector of Dallas so that they could receive visibility, possible funding, volunteers, and serve as a resource for funders to become aware of these agencies through the ServeSouthernDallas.org website. Network Guardians try to create win-win opportunities for all involved in the network through programs or services as previously mentioned.

Here is a checklist to determine what kind of network weaver you are.

Network Weaver Checklist by Roles by June Holley

What kind of Network Weaver are you? Mark each from one to five, with five being "major strength" and one being "lack this quality."[4]

Weaver or Connector

1. Loves to unearth other people's dreams and visions, strengths, and gifts

2. Helps people identify challenges and introduce them to others who can help

3. Encourages people with skills and resources to connect to people with needs

4. Models an approach to relationships that is positive, appreciative, and focused on strengths and gifts

5. Treats everyone as a peer

6. Encourages complex reciprocity—sharing information & resources with others without expecting a return from that person because you know others will share with you

7. Points out the value of knowing people with different perspectives and from different backgrounds

8. Encourages people to listen deeply to each other

9.   Encourages people to identify shared or overlapping interests or values

10. Helps people make accurate and realistic assessments of others

11. Helps people bring innovation and new perspectives into their network by adding new people to their network

Collaborative Project Coordinator

1.   Initiates cross-organizational collaborations and activities with others

2.   Shows people how to build trust through small, low-risk collaborations with others

3.   Has good project coordination skills

4.   Encourages initial collaborations to be "small acts" or projects

5.   Not attached to specific next steps but enjoys helping people do something

6.   Encourages people to see conflicts as opportunities to develop breakthroughs

7.   Helps people reflect on successes and failures and understand the underlying "patterns of success"

8.   Quickly helps people see when something doesn't work and move on

9.   Insists that people check assumptions about what others are saying

10. Encourages people to share about their project with larger networks

11. Encourages others to initiate cross-organizational collaborations and activities and provide coaching for them

Network Facilitator or Organizer

1.   Convene people with common interests to form a network

2.   Continually unearths new people with needed skills, resources, and perspectives and link them into the network

3.   Helps people map, analyze and enhance their networks

4.   Helps people understand smart networks concepts and translate them into practice

5.   Helps network determine strategic directions

6.   Helps small projects move to scale

7.   Encourages more people to become Network Weavers

8.   Sets up training and coaching for Network Weavers and project coordinators

9.   Finds resources to support the functioning of the network

10.   Sets up communications systems for the network

Network Guardian

1.   Supports, encourages and mentors Network Weavers

2.   Encourages others to become Network Weavers and take responsibility for increasing the health of their networks

3.   Helps the network identify and enhance or set up networking hubs or spaces where people can run into each other

4.   Helps people reflect on successes and failures and understand the underlying "patterns of success"

5.   Sees patterns in the network: where there is energy, where there is isolation, and help develop strategies to deal with those aspects of the network

6.   Communicates about networks to the public

7.   Makes sure that network weavers and network projects are celebrated in the local media

8.   Sets up an innovation fund to provide seed funds for small collaborations

9.   Finds or provides resources for networks and training for Network Weavers

The highest score will determine which role you may play in your network(s). This wonderful tool was adapted from the work of June Holley. I have listed her book as a resource that I would strongly encourage you to obtain if you want to know more about networking weaving. This is important because many of us do not see our networks through our personal and professional affiliations as a tool for change. This is an opportunity to begin to leverage these relationships differently using your social capital and address the gaps in assets that exist in a community. Your relationships may be the key to solve for an issue in your area! As a philanthropist, this is another way to give of your time, talent, and treasure.

Narrative Change: So often in communities, taking credit is important for those who are involved in being a part of the change. Taking credit, without being inclusive of those who also support the project, is disingenuous. It is important that in our work, we are collaborating and bringing others with us. For me, it is always thinking about creating a pipeline of leadership and recognizing those who are participating. The narrative must move from being about "me" to focus on "we."

One of the things that I've been careful about is making sure that we are not serving as the lead in the projects I've mentioned in my work. Distributed leadership is so important, and when working in communities it is critical that indigenous leadership is in a position of power. It is also important to note that if something happens to me or my team, the work can continue to exist without me because of my intentionality of sharing information and empowering others to lead. If you are coming from the outside to help in a community, it is a disservice to the individuals and organizations in those areas if you start something and cannot maintain it. If the work is solely dependent upon you for its existence, that is a problem. Make sure that as you are connecting others to networks or establishing them you are clear on your role of being a catalyst and not a controller. Networks exist in not only affluent communities but in under-resourced areas as well. When we see the power of these within communities and add our gifts and talents as a compliment, transformation is inevitable.

Call to Action: *You can be a Network Weaver!* Begin to think about the individuals that you know. Use the chart below to serve as a guide to identifying individuals that are in your network that could be resources for your community? Could they be tapped to assist an individual, an organization, or even help you with a project you are working on like the creation of a giving circle? Make a list of five to ten individuals in each category that you can tap into their gifts and talents to make a difference. As you review the roles of the Network Weaver, who will fill each role (Connector, Facilitator, Coordinator, or Network Guardian) in your network?

Directions: Begin to map your network. Think about your circle of influence and the talents or possibilities for each.

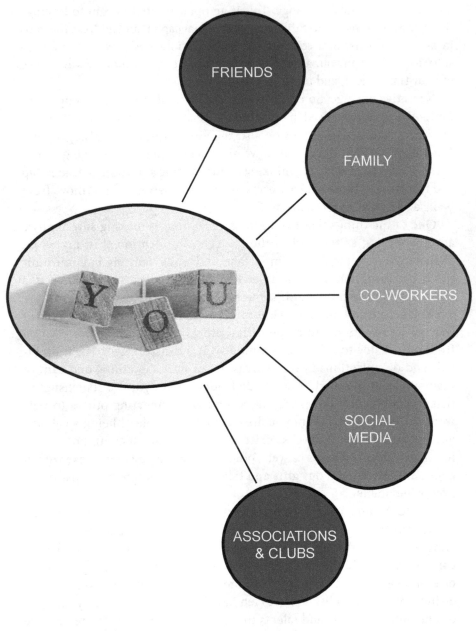

Circle of Influence[5]

Scripture to Ponder

1 Corinthians 12:4-30 (NIV) summarizes this entire section so well:

[4] There are different kinds of gifts, but the same Spirit distributes them. [5] There are different kinds of service, but the same Lord. [6] There are different kinds of working, but in all of them and in everyone it is the same God at work.

[7] Now to each one the manifestation of the Spirit is given for the common good. [8] To one there is given through the Spirit a message of wisdom, to another a message of knowledge by means of the same Spirit, [9] to another faith by the same Spirit, to another gifts of healing by that one Spirit, [10] to another miraculous powers, to another prophecy, to another distinguishing between spirits, to another speaking in different kinds of tongues, and to still another the interpretation of tongues. [11] All these are the work of one and the same Spirit, and he distributes them to each one, just as he determines.

[12] Just as a body, though one, has many parts, but all its many parts form one body, so it is with Christ. [13] For we were all baptized by one Spirit so as to form one body—whether Jews or Gentiles, slave or free—and we were all given the one Spirit to drink. [14] Even so the body is not made up of one part but of many.

[15] Now if the foot should say, "Because I am not a hand, I do not belong to the body," it would not for that reason stop being part of the body. [16] And if the ear should say, "Because I am not an eye, I do not belong to the body," it would not for that reason stop being part of the body. [17] If the whole body were an eye, where would the sense of hearing be? If the whole body were an ear, where would the sense of smell be? [18] But in fact God has placed the parts in the body, every one of them, just as he wanted them to be. [19] If they were all one part, where would the body be? [20] As it is, there are many parts, but one body.

[21] The eye cannot say to the hand, "I don't need you!" And the head cannot say to the feet, "I don't need you!" [22] On the contrary, those parts of the body that seem to be weaker are indispensable, [23] and the parts that we think are less honorable we treat with special honor. And the parts that are unpresentable are treated with special modesty, [24] while our presentable parts need no special treatment. But God has put the body together, giving greater honor to the parts that lacked it, [25] so that there should be no division in the body, but that its parts should have equal concern for each other. [26] If one part suffers, every part suffers with it; if one part is honored, every part rejoices with it.

[27] Now you are the body of Christ, and each one of you is a part of it. [28] And God has placed in the church first of all apostles, second prophets, third teachers, then miracles, then gifts of healing, of helping, of guidance, and

of different kinds of tongues. [29] Are all apostles? Are all prophets? Are all teachers? Do all work miracles? [30] Do all have gifts of healing? Do all speak in tongues? Do all interpret? [31] Now eagerly desire the greater gifts.

There is such diversity, in addition to our race, gender, class, and other identities, that exists within our community. God has given each of us talents and gifts that are to compliment the body of Christ. We must begin to change the narrative that focuses on limitations instead of seeing the possibilities that exist within all of us. God has something for each of us to do and it is equally as important. No one should be left behind because everyone matters and so does every community. How does this Scripture resonate with you for your organization, company, church, or community?

16

ANALYZING SYSTEMS AND
THE POST-COVID-19 IMPACT

The reason we started HERitage Giving Circle was to make sure that the organizations led by Black women, which were often overlooked by mainstream philanthropic efforts, were receiving the funding they needed to operate. The nonprofit sector has been challenged with bias and racism just as other parts of our society. Based on a subset of data from a 2016 and a 2018 Race to Lead survey,[1] as well as focus groups and interviews with nonprofit CEOs and executive directors of color, the report *Nonprofit Executives and the Racial Leadership Gap: A Race to Lead Brief* found that executives of color reported leadership challenges and frustrations such as being called on to represent a community, inadequate compensation, lack of relationships with funding sources, lack of social capital, and lack of role models at higher rates than their White peers. In focus groups and interviews, leaders of color, especially women, also mentioned the pressures of their workload resulted in negative health outcomes. In addition to this data collected from the study, they discovered that "white-led organizations often benefited from more diversified funding sources, including government contracts, individual donors, and fees-for-service."[2] White-led organizations often have access to more information about funding opportunities, social capital, and financial resources than Black-led organizations. *Black-led organizations, especially those led by women, face enormous challenges. We realized during COVID that our strategy had to be different because the needs for our organizations changed. As donors, examining these past issues along with this new reality will be important as we move forward.*

Systems thinking is critical to solving complex issues. It allows us to think about patterns, interrelated parts, and structures that are at work. In doing this, we can minimize the amount of money used, time wasted, and talent that was misapplied to solve a problem.

> Systems thinking often involves moving from observing events or data, to identifying patterns of behavior overtime, to surfacing the underlying structures that drive those events and patterns. By understanding and changing structures that are not serving us well (including our mental models and perceptions), we can expand the choices available to us and create more satisfying, long-term solutions to chronic problems.[3]

So often, we fail to analyze the systems that play a significant role in placing people in positions that are out of their control. This does not remove accountability and responsibility, however. Some consider it to be either this or that response and quite frankly, we must consider both. We must consider not only the personal level of responsibility but the role that society plays in these systems. We must also consider when there is a benefit for some and not for all. When we are silent about these systems, is it because there is a fear of loss by speaking up against something that we believe is bigger than we are? Nehemiah reminds us that in rebuilding the wall, we cannot be afraid to interact with the secular to make a difference for the sacred (Nehemiah 1:1-10). There must be a reckoning to evaluate and dismantle ways of thinking and doing that is harmful and oppressive to entire populations of people.

The ramifications of these systems take a toll. Our historical and cultural past has not ended. The impact of racism, exclusion and segregation has had an impact in every area of our lives.

In chapter 13, I discuss briefly the systems that many BIPOCs encounter, such as criminal justice, healthcare, and education that have created challenges because of a lack of relationships, power, and race. It is important when working in communities that you are aware of the differences that BIPOCs may face that are very different than the experiences of Whites in America.

In previous chapters, some of the disparities pre-COVID were listed. Here are a few more to demonstrate the issues that exist in wealth, education, and incarceration:

- For every $100 a White family earns, a Black family earns $57.30.[4]

- Black-sounding names are often not called back for job interviews.

- Whites and Blacks with identical resumes will still result in 50 percent more callbacks for Whites.[5]

- Education is another area with huge discrepancies: 47 percent of Black males graduate from high school.[6]

- According to the Schott Foundation, "In most states it is easier for the public to track the number of Black and Latino males who are incarcerated than the number who graduate from high school in any given year."[7]

- A Black person is five times more likely to be stopped without just cause than a White person. On average, Black Americans are exposed to four police killings of other unarmed Black Americans in the same state each year. African Americans are incarcerated at more than five times the rate of Whites.[8]

The pre-existing inequalities and barriers are now compounded as we move to a world that looks forward to life after the pandemic. Post-COVID-19 philanthropy must be aware of the challenges that are exacerbating these existing realities for Black and Brown people. As individual donors or even those within corporate or foundation spaces, it will be imperative to examine the impact of these issues before creating new plans. It will require systems thinking. This is comparable to an iceberg. If we only see the top part of the ice without examining what is below the water, we are missing a clear view of what we need to address to move forward.

Less than one in five black workers and roughly one in six Hispanic workers are able to work from home

Share of workers who can telework, by race and ethnicity, 2017–2018

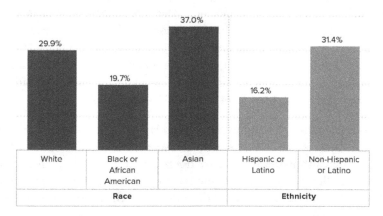

Source: U.S. Bureau of Labor Statistics, Job Flexibilities and Work Schedules — 2017–2018 Data from the American Time Use Survey

Economic Policy Institute

It's easy to mistake our circumstances as the reality for most. For many of us in professional roles, we had options during the pandemic. This wasn't the case for many individuals who were unable to work from home. For many of those individuals who work in retail, logistics, or construction, working from home was not an option. When schools were being closed due to the pandemic, many young people were in communities that did not have internet access. Parents who worked from home were more than likely to have jobs that could be moved to working from home, and lived in areas that already had internet access. "Broadband adoption rates in Black and Latino or Hispanic households lag behind white households by 6.8% and 3.4%, respectively. Further, when Black and Latino or Hispanic households do have in-home broadband, they're more likely than white households to rely only on mobile connections."[9] As the world becomes more technologically advanced and jobs become more digital, Black and Brown families will suffer because of a lack of access. This is an opportunity for each of us to think strategically about how we can support communities with hotspots, broadband access, hardware, and software along with training to help provide skills that will move people into better employment opportunities and ensure that young people are not further left behind when we return to some sense of normalcy in the years to come.

The achievement gap is real for low-income youth, and because of COVID-19, the issues for Black and Hispanic children will have a significant impact for years to come. According to McKinsey and Company,

> Learning loss will probably be greatest among low-income, black, and Hispanic students. Data from Curriculum Associates, creators of the i-Ready digital-instruction and -assessment software, suggest that only 60 percent of low-income students are regularly logging into online instruction; 90 percent of high-income students do. Engagement rates are also lagging behind in schools serving predominantly black and Hispanic students; just 60 to 70 percent are logging in regularly. Black students may fall behind by 10.3 months, Hispanic students by 9.2 months, and low-income students by more than a year. We estimate that this would exacerbate existing achievement gaps by 15 to 20 percent.[10]

In addition, dropout rates for both Black and Hispanic students are expected to rise. The social isolation that students have experienced will also contribute to mental health issues that we are not prepared to address. These issues are serious challenges but can become real opportunities for nonprofits and churches to support existing agencies doing work in these communities to address these unforeseen consequences of the virus.

FIGURE 1

Share of households with school-aged children who have wired high-speed internet at home

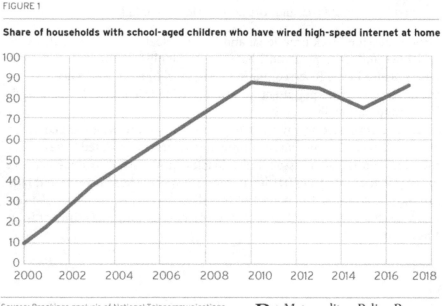

Source: Brookings analysis of National Telecommunications
and Information Administration data

B | Metropolitan Policy Program
   at BROOKINGS

In addition to the issues that a lack of technology presented, mental health is another area that goes without much discussion and even less treatment in communities of color, especially within the Black community. Pre-COVID, there were already challenges related to mental health. Mental Health America (MHA) shares startling statistics about the number of Black people in the United States who deal with mental illness, much of it due to racism and oppression. MHA states,

> Historical adversity, which includes slavery, sharecropping, and race-based exclusion from health, educational, social, and economic resources, translates into socioeconomic disparities experienced by Black and African American people today. Socioeconomic status, in turn, is linked to mental health: people who are impoverished, homeless, incarcerated, or have substance use problems are at higher risk for poor mental health. Despite progress made over the years, racism continues to have an impact on the mental health of Black and African American people. Negative stereotypes and attitudes of rejection have decreased, but continue to occur with measurable, adverse consequences. Historical and contemporary instances of negative treatment have led

to a mistrust of authorities, many of whom are not seen as having the best interests of Black and African Americans in mind.[11]

Groups like the Black Emotional and Mental Health Collective (BEAM)[12] and Loveland Therapy Fund[13] have been established to address mental health issues in the Black community. There will be more of a need in the future for funders to pay attention to supporting initiatives like these both locally and nationally.

As I've witnessed in my work in South Dallas, the issues are complex and multifaceted. It's not just one thing but several interrelated issues. Mass incarceration is also an issue in the Black community. This issue became exacerbated during COVID, due to multiple outbreaks at prisons and jails around the country. The impact of this disease on the prison population, and what happens when they return to their communities, is still not fully known or discussed.

COVID-19 INFECTIONS IN JAILS UNDER CURRENT RESPONSE

Jails could see more infections, hospitalizations, and deaths under the current response. These higher infection rates could spill over into the broader community.

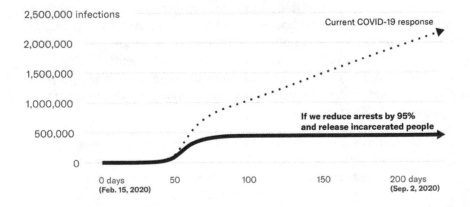

Note: Estimates of infections are cumulative, and jail staff are included in count. "Current response" refers to the shelter in place orders in effect as of April 13, 2020. We recommend stopping 95% of arrests — all but the most serious crimes — and doubling the rate of release for those currently detained.

A dear friend is currently housed in a facility in the Texas Department of Criminal Justice as a trustee. Per our calls, there have been numerous outbreaks with reports of over four hundred inmates who have been affected. Even as they quarantine individuals, there is too little space for social distancing, and the lack of resources for healthcare is limited at many facilities. Resources, such as masks, are available but there are limited supplies of hand sanitizer. What happens when many of these men and women return home without access to healthcare to address the possible aftermath of the disease compounded with pre-existing conditions that many have such as high blood pressure, asthma, or obesity? We must face the reality for the Black community after COVID and how collaborative support can make a difference. For those individuals who return from prison or even those frontline workers who have experienced this disease, we may not know the issues they will face for years to come.

The number of deaths due to COVID-19 in the Black community is staggering. One example is the loss of a twenty-one-year-old who was a kind, gentle spirit with so much to offer our world. On December 18 at 12:32 a.m., Chris Miller[14] passed away from COVID-19 complications. I have known Chris since he was a toddler. He was a senior at Austin College and was diagnosed with the disease in August. Chris spent months in ICU. After being on a ventilator and multiple battles with blood clots, he was released to go home. Once Chris came home, he began to have breathing issues and needed surgery. Chris' mother and I have been close friends for years and his death impacted me deeply. It is stories like Chris that are constant.

Even with the numerous vaccines that are available, for those who have experienced this disease, we will not know its impact for years. Families have lost loved ones that provided support. Companies have lost employees. Communities have lost members that were contributors. The loss of more than five hundred thousand individuals will also have an impact economically, mentally, and emotionally for decades. Our healthcare system and funders must be prepared to think futuristically to plan for the challenges. In order to have any level of success, it will require systems thinking.

Narrative Change: In Chinese, the word "crisis" is sometimes misquoted to mean "opportunity." The first character, *wēi* (危), means dangerous but the second character, *jī* (机; 機), means change point. A crisis is indeed an opportunity for change. As we have witnessed social injustice in the murders of George Floyd, Breonna Taylor, and many others in addition to COVID-19's surge across the world, we have the chance to change the narrative. How can we rethink, reimagine, or rebuild/destroy those things that no longer serve our communities well? How can we work collaboratively regardless of

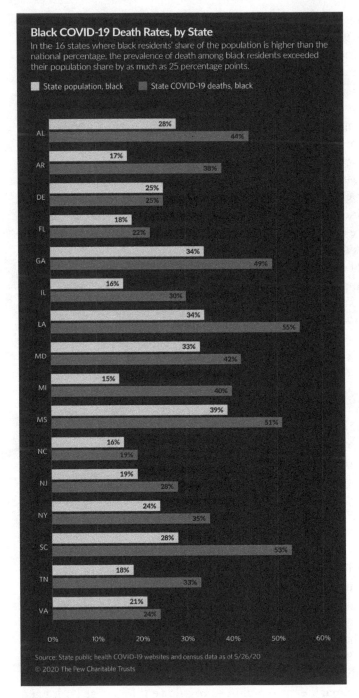

Covid Deaths[15]

denomination, race, or ideology to make changes that create equitable conditions? We can't do this on faith alone. It's time to join in the work that is going on in communities of color across the country. "But someone will say, 'You have faith and I have works.' Show me your faith apart from your works, and I will show you my faith by my works" (James 2:18 ESV).

Call to Action: COVID-19 must push us to think differently about the role systems play in the lives of Black Americans. Those issues that existed prior to the pandemic will become more pronounced. There are real opportunities for strategic and systems thinking using our networks and assets to address these issues. It is also an opportunity to re-examine our funding focus to address many of these issues with an infusion of resources. As a result of COVID-19, we know that the following changes have occurred and will continue:

- Changes in the workplace

- Increased use of technology

- The way we connect to one another in public

What does this mean for the way you work in communities and partner? How will this possibly change your giving in the near future? Is there an opportunity to create a giving circle using your network to support these efforts?

17

RECOGNIZING THE ROLE OF POWER DYNAMICS

When I worked for World Vision, I became keenly aware of the difference between agreement and compliance. Many individuals and nonprofits who work in under-resourced areas tend to believe that because people are working with them that it suggests agreement. They do not know or recognize the power they have or how those who need the resources will often comply just to have access. There is a big difference between the two. This concept became solidified for me when I visited India. I remember that we encountered several individuals who would nod their heads as if they were agreeing with our statements. I later discovered that it was not agreement but more of a physical expression of saying I hear you. When you are unaware of cultural dynamics, it is so easy to assume that you understand, when in reality, there is so much that you fail to understand. Since those experiences, I recognize my power and my privilege when I am bringing resources to an area.

One of the most profound books I have read is *Reframing Organizations: Artistry, Choice, and Leadership* by authors Lee G. Bolman and Terrence E. Deal. The book reveals that there are frames that exist in organizations. These frames serve as a lens that we filter our experiences and information within organizations. I would add that these frames also exist within communities but in a different context. The first frame is the structural frame, which is rules, policies, and procedures. Within communities, it is important to be aware of how things have been done, who are the stakeholders as well as those who serve as the 'old guard' (guardians) that are the leaders even sometimes unofficially in an area. When one of my team members first started at the State Fair, it was important that I introduced her to those who not only had formal authority but those who were not on the radar but were well respected, often elders, in the area. It is important to know them, gain historical perspective, and listen. I also encourage individuals working within communities to meet with both those who are the established leadership and those who are the up-and-coming movers and shakers. We often dismiss youth and young leaders, and it is critical that they are a part of the process of change in an area. Otherwise, we miss out on the opportunity to learn from them and to be a part of their journey as mentors, colleagues, and friends. It is important to pay attention to roles within communities and how things operate first before bringing ideas on what needs to happen. There is usually a system that is in place and although it may not align with your beliefs or how you are accustomed to doing things, our role is to come alongside instead of lead.

The political frame or lens according to Boleman and Deal is about the power dynamics that exist within organizations. Communities also deal with power dynamics. We tend to assume that power is connected to wealth and resources and this is not true. Power struggles also exist in under-resourced areas. Because opportunities are often limited, people fight even harder to gain access to being involved, seen, or heard. Different interests are competing for funding and often, because of the challenges to secure dollars, nonprofits will often compete heavily against one another in some communities for resources. I don't blame communities for this. Donors must begin to work diligently to level the playing field and to not just focus on the golden organization of a community but commit to pouring dollars into a neighborhood or a community as well as build their capacity so that they are sustainable for the long-term. Creating competition not only hurts the organizations, but the communities suffer as well because of the scavenger or lack mentality that is created by those from the outside. As an organization or entity seeking to support a community-based nonprofit, the goal is not to create a scarcity model but one that empowers each organization by committing long-term to their success and providing resources beyond dollars while introducing new networks and assets to the conversation. It is about the redistribution of power from those outside the community to those within the area. So many communities suffer from brain drain when those who lived in the community at one time move, especially if they were in a position of power with resources. The problem becomes that power was wrongly concentrated and did not stay in the hands of those most invested—the people who live there!

The human relations lens or frame in an organization focuses on people, empowerment, and support. Organizations and communities can run like families. Many neighborhood leaders are seen as grandparents or aunts of the community, especially in Black communities. Relationships are very different than what may be standard in other areas. This may also become frustrating for those who are eager to come into communities but feel as though the people are slow-moving and unresponsive. Early in my career, I had no clue of what was going on when I was invited to meeting after meeting regarding an issue. What I thought should have taken one call or email resulted in multiple meetings. I soon realized that this was more about relationship building and cultivating trust than closing a deal. For those who are coming in from corporate backgrounds, without a knowledge of how time and relationships move in communities, it can become aggravating. This lack of understanding creates division and generates stereotypes that are damaging. Relationships require communication (lots of listening), trust, and an investment of time in communities, too.

The final frame of Boleman and Deal is the symbolic frame which focuses on the history, culture, rituals, ceremonies, and unspoken elements that exist within an organization. This too exists within communities. It is critical to pay attention to not just what we see but the "water cooler" conversations that exist within communities. So much of history isn't necessarily in a textbook that we can learn from listening to people's stories. Stories are crucial assets in communities. When prejudice, unconscious bias, and racism are not addressed, they can show up in the way we interact with communities through our decision-making for funding, the creation of policies, or even who we chose to work with. It takes time to eliminate bias and it requires being open and listening. I realize that even though I have done extensive work and know about South Dallas, or even about my home in Shreveport, Louisiana, there is still so much I do not know. Posturing from a position of a student is necessary as we work to learn more about an organization or an area. When I was working on my PhD, one of the first things we were told was to share our positionality.

> Positionality is the notion that personal values, views, and location in time and space influence how one understands the world. In this context, gender, race, class, and other aspects of identities are indicators of social and spatial positions and are not fixed, given qualities. Positions act on the knowledge a person has about things, both material and abstract. Consequently, knowledge is the product of a specific position that reflects particular places and spaces.[1]

Knowing our positionality also helps us to recognize our power and how it may impact our views, how we see others, and the way they may experience us.

Positionality forces each of us to own our identities and realize how they shape our behavior and how we see the world and others. As we focus on the importance of owning our identities, it's important to better understand the role of intersectionality in our identities. The concept of intersectionality was coined in the early 1990s by legal scholar Kimberlé Crenshaw (1991), whose research explores the categories of race, gender, class, ability, and sexual orientation that often shape the employment, political, and structural experiences that women of color encounter. I am a Black woman who has a PhD which places me in a unique class that has power attached to it. Yet, being Black and a woman places me in groups that are marginalized. Intersectionality provides a lens on how identities can impact our social mobility and resources. As we explore intersectionality in our identities, it is important to note the power (or lack of power) attached to them.

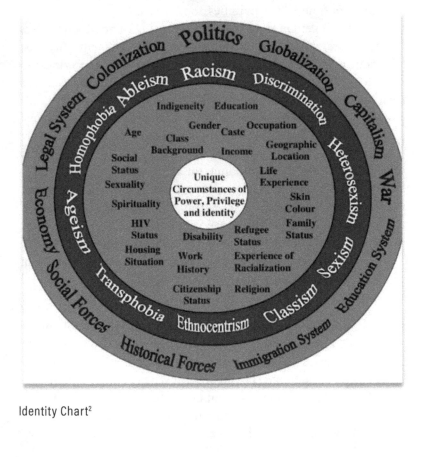

Identity Chart[2]

As we work in communities, think about how all our identities and lived experiences shape our narratives and the narratives of our neighborhoods. When we recognize our power or the lack thereof in many individuals, organizations, and communities, we can then move from noticing what's wrong to how we can use what we have as leverage to make a difference. "Intersectionality encourages recognition of the differences that exist among groups, moving dialogue beyond considering only the differences between groups."[3]

Narrative Change: Power is not a bad thing but using it to intentionally or unintentionally harm others is the problem. It is important that we own our identities. If your identity is a part of a group that has been dominant and oppressive, it doesn't mean that you hide from it. It is an opportunity to use that power to be different and do something different. It is an opportunity to connect with others to serve as an ally, advocate, resource, and my favorite—a co-conspirator—to those who may not have access to the power and possibilities that you do. As an individual interested in making a difference, we cannot hide from the role power plays but what we can do is speak truth to power when it is abusive and controlling in the lives of individuals, organizations, and communities. It may seem impossible, but we know that "with God all things are possible" (Matthew 19:26 ESV). "Finally, brothers, rejoice. Aim for restoration, comfort one another, agree with one another, live in peace; and the God of love and peace will be with you" (2 Corinthians 13:11 ESV).

Call to Action: Scripture calls us to renew our minds. ". . . but be transformed by the renewal of your mind . . ." (Romans 12:2 NIV). As we think of the frames by Boleman and Deal, this requires us to think differently about others. It is important that we are aware of our power and how power dynamics impact our communities. As you review the four frames listed previously, how do you see these in your organization? In your church? In your job? What are your identities using the chart as a guide? How does this shape your lived experience and positionality?

18

LIVING LIVES OF EMPATHY

'll never forget Harriet Schwartz. She was a student at Antioch University with me. One day during our residency, she encouraged me to attend a conference on Relational Cultural Theory (RCT). I remember researching this theory and finding the resources to attend the conference at Wellesley College in Boston. It was there that I met the renowned Drs. Judith Jordan, Karen Craddock, Maureen Walker, and Amy Banks. Harriet not only shared RCT with me, but she also embodied the concepts in her interaction with me and others. Harriet and I have worked together since serving as affiliate faculty at Antioch University. In one of our conversations, she shared her experiences as a Jewish woman and the fear she has faced, especially when a mass shooting occurred at the Tree of Life Synagogue in Pittsburgh in 2018, which is close to where she lives. She noted that the experience created fear for her life, and at that moment, she recognized that this must be something that her Black friends experience daily. Harriet immediately clarified that her goal was not to make a comparison or to lessen the experience—it was to demonstrate empathy. As we work in marginalized communities, empathy is critical. We must be willing to not feel the need to justify our experiences but to find compassion in the stories and narratives of others. Harriet did that. Hearing her story also did the same thing for me. I didn't know exactly how she felt, but I experienced compassion for her. We need more opportunities for listening, for connecting, for compassion, and for empathy when we are working with others. RTC is a tool that I believe can move us in that direction.

RTC evolved from the work of Jean Baker Miller and others who noticed that the issues and perspectives of their female clients were not being addressed in therapy and in literature. RTC states that "people grow through action in relation to one another," and people seek for "connection with others throughout the lifespan"[1] In Relational Cultural Theory, growth fostering relationships are a critical component. These relationships are built on mutually beneficial connections. So often, we experience disconnection and isolation in society causing separation and the inability to be truly authentic. The concept of the separate self is significant in Relational Cultural Theory. In our society, we are conditioned from our childhood to create distance from our parents so that we can become independent instead of interdependent. We yearn for connections and yet, we are afraid of being vulnerable and not accepted. When we are in growth fostering relationships, we experience the "Five Good Things":

1. Each person feels a greater sense of zest (vitality, energy)

2. Each person feels more able to act and does act in the world

3. Each person has a more accurate picture of her/himself and the other person(s)

4. Each person feels a greater sense of worth

5. Each person feels more connected to other persons and exhibits a greater motivation to connect with other people beyond those in one's primary relationships.[2]

It is more than just a feeling. There are tangible results to building empathy and relationships.

There are multiple markers of good connections because of the "Five Good Things":

- Engagement
- Empathy
- Mutual Empathy
- Relational Authenticity
- Mutuality
- Difference/Diversity
- Empowerment and Mutual Empowerment

When we create spaces for connection, people are willing to become more involved. As they are in proximity to one another, they experience empathy for others and can begin to see themselves in the stories of others. Diversity is valued and appreciated along with the desire to see others excel and grow.

The idea of labeling others as different moves to a new perspective from the label of "them" to "we."

In my work at the State Fair of Texas, I've been very intentional about embedding the Five Good Things in my work:

1. There is a natural drive toward relationships in our collaborations and convenings.

My team is small, but we are able to accomplish so much because of the focus on building our partners. We convene nonprofits through our Community Engagement Days which are opportunities to build social capital. Many agencies often say they need funding, and I reply that you need a relationship. These convenings are designed to help organizations identify existing assets in their community to reduce the duplication of services but also facilitate relationship building. From these events, I've seen organizations grow their programs through partnerships. I've seen the sharing of resources like vehicles to the use of space for events. None of this could happen without relationships.

2. Mutual growth fostering is a result of the advocacy, trainings, and cohorts that we provide.

Instead of solely focusing on how our needs are met, we listen to our neighbors to learn how we can help these organizations grow. We have advocated for transportation, criminal justice reform, the census, and other issues that were of importance to our neighbors. In doing this, it not only built their capacity but also assisted in our growth as a valued, trusted partner. In doing this, we've *created positive relational experiences rooted in trust.*

3. Energy and productivity increased (due to ownership).

We believe in empowering our neighbors. All our programs depend upon partners at the table sharing their experiences and ideas as we support them. People are willing to be engaged when they know that their voices matter and that they are supported.

4. Clarity due to increased knowledge of self, organization, and community.

Our work is about empowerment and through initiatives like Leadership Circles that we have hosted through our United Way/State Fair Infrastructure Initiative or through HERitage Giving Circle. These leadership circles are opportunities for leaders to reflect, share, support, and strategize on how to help one another. They learn from each other in these safe spaces for conversations about issues they face in their work.

5. Increase in worth

Our goal in our work is to change the narrative in philanthropy. We value and support organizations led by BIPOCs through our financial, social, and human capital investments. This has resulted in partnerships with Corporate and Private Foundations to serve as a resource as they identify who to work with within our community.

As a funder, such as for the State Fair of Texas, or through a giving circle, such as HERitage Giving Circle, knowing our power is important in communities, which is why we work hard to share power with those we support. Power dynamics are also an important theme in RCT as mentioned in the previous chapter. It is not focused on "power over" but rather "power with" in relationships.[3] If a person uses their power in a relationship to dominate, it is about control. This does not create space for "supported vulnerability, mutual empathetic involvement . . . and creating meaning in more relational awareness."[4] If we are going to impact our communities differently and in collaboration with indigenous leadership, we must lead and serve with empathy. Our goal should be to help others see the power that exists within them and work with them to share power that is not violent or abusive but uplifts them to fulfill God's purpose and plan for their lives and their communities.

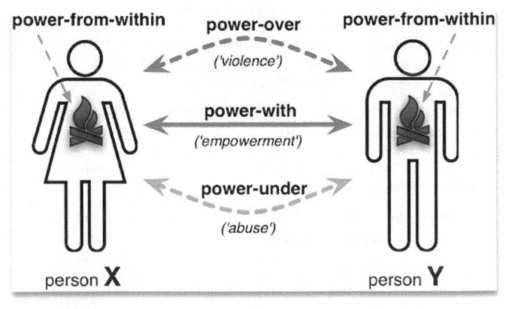

Power Chart[5]

Narrative Change: Cognitive dissonance is something we need more of. "Cognitive dissonance can make people feel uneasy and uncomfortable, particularly if the disparity between their beliefs and behaviors involves something that is central to their sense of self. For example, behaving in ways that are not aligned with your personal values may result in intense feelings of discomfort."[6] Instead of running from those experiences or desiring to be right, it's time that we sit in our discomfort and wrestle with why something makes us feel uneasy. We need to ask ourselves why do we feel like we are losing something and why is it okay that others can't win with us? We must be willing to address our discomfort with empathy instead of retreat, sarcasm, and justification of why we feel the way we do. While working in communities that are different than ours, the goal is not to confirm what we already believe but to challenge our thinking and be open to the possibilities even if it means discomfort and growth. There is a wonderful illustration of empathy—a person falls into a pit. A person who is sympathetic yells down and says, "I hope you are okay" and walks away. A person who is empathetic crawls down into the pit with the person. Are you in the pit with those who have fallen or are you just walking by hoping that someone else comes to the rescue?

Call to Action: As much as action is a significant part of this book, reflection is equally as important. There is a scholar by the name of Schon[7] whose work focuses on critical reflection. He states that as we make meaning of experiences, it is necessary to be aware of our knowledge and lived experiences while also having the willingness to reframe our experiences. My goal with this book is to provide a framework for engaging in philanthropy, community development, and with diverse communities. As you read this work, I hope that you are open to a new lens as well as reflecting critically on what you've read. Schön states that we should do the following:

- "reflect-on-action"
  (examining past experience)

- "reflect-in-action"
  (when a situation is occurring)

- "reflect-for-action"
  (paying attention to how to proceed in the future)

As you think about interacting with different people or communities, how has empathy played (or not) a role in your decision-making and actions? Think about past experiences. What did you do? What could you do differently? What could be enhanced? In the future, when a situation is occurring, how can you be more empathetic, open, and willing to listen even when it is very different than your lifestyle or point of view? How will you move forward in the future when you are faced with differing opinions, attitudes, lifestyles, thinking, or experiences? How will empathy show up and are there opportunities to use RCT to create more enriching and positive relationships?

The work of Narrative 4 is compelling. This organization is using the power of storytelling to impact the way we interact with those who are different. "Narrative 4 is a global organization driven by artists, shaped by educators and led by students. Our core methodology, the story exchange, is designed to help students understand that their voices, stories, actions and lives matter, and that they have the power to change, rebuild and revolutionize systems."[8] I would encourage you to check out their work—even though it is for students; it can offer so much to adults who see the power of narrative and identity as an opportunity to create change.

19

LEADING (AND FOLLOWING) IS CRITICAL IN RELATIONSHIPS

I was given the opportunity to visit a wonderful community in Georgia that provides comprehensive services for mixed-income communities. It was a fascinating trip to witness work that included housing, recreational services, and a school. I was a part of a group that was exploring bringing this concept to the South Dallas area. As impressive as this work is, I realized very quickly that low-income communities have similarities as well as unique dynamics that only they may face. Believing that we could adopt the same concept as is and bring it to our area would be delusional and irresponsible. There were components that were scalable to our community, but it was necessary to consider the historical, cultural, and social dynamics that were critical to the success of this project. There were many organizational leaders involved in this project. One of the things I have learned in my years of being involved in community development is knowing when I can direct and lead but also being aware of when I need to step back, listen, and be okay with not being in a position of power. In the situation in Georgia, I realized very quickly my role as a contributor but not as one in a position to dictate what could happen.

For many, it is so easy to begin to dictate what we've done in the past and lead with our resumes. We feel that it is important to establish credibility up front. In my experience, it's important to analyze the audience first. Proving to a group of neighborhood leaders that I'm highly educated when we are there to listen about a new highway coming through the area doesn't establish credibility. It lends itself to establishing dominance. I see myself as one who serves when I enter communities and not one who feels I need to position myself as an expert but as one who walks with those who are there. It is my role to listen and learn.

In so many communities of color, including South Dallas, organizations that partner with local agencies will take credit for the work of those who are on the ground. They will use the work of those they are helping to then collect funds for their own organizations which never goes to the individuals doing the work. There are some groups who go to events and then claim that they had a part in the planning of the event which is misleading, especially if the outside organization shows up for pictures only to promote their involvement. These groups had no part in the recruitment, relationships, or work and used it to garner additional funding and support. It is all under the guise to help, but it ultimately harms those organizations who are invested in those communities and sometimes causes them to lose funding and visibility because others are riding on their work claiming it as their own. It's unethical and it's unfair. I'll never forget one evening receiving a text from a local nonprofit leader who needed guidance. She was frustrated because an organization wanted to partner with her. They knew she had relationships in the community and wanted to bring resources to support her. She recruited the participants and even participated in the logistics. The event was held at her facility and was a success. Later, she found out that the organization did not mention their partnership, created marketing materials that excluded her involvement, and gave the impression that they did all of the work, had relationships in this community, and it was their program. This happens more often than ever shared or discussed because of power dynamics. Who wants to lose relationships that have access to resources to help those you serve?

The confusion begins in communities with well-meaning individuals because of different agendas and expectations. Having a shared language is important and critical to avoid misalignment of priorities. "Our inability to have a shared language that allows us to create meaning together influences the way we connect to one another."[1] "Being receives much of its power from connectedness."[2] It is important that we are honest and provide clarity about our intentions, agenda, and expectations early. If you are going to share content about a group or your work with them, always ask them to review it especially if the relationship is very young and not established. They should have a say in how they are promoted, discussed, or included in your work.

Linda Tuhiwai Smith's book *Decolonizing Methodologies: Research and Indigenous Peoples* discusses the role of Western colonization and the impact it has had on indigenous cultures and research on these groups. One of the most profound memories I have of this book is her discussion of artifacts in museums. Until that time, I never really paid attention to who these items belonged to. Many of these items were stolen by researchers and historians who took them to other parts of the world to study and analyze, but they were not familiar with the people or the cultural context. As a result, they used their limited interactions to then create a narrative that did not involve the perspective and experience of the tribes these materials were taken from. She states,

> For example, there were a number of books published in the nineteenth century which told the stories of life in the New Zealand colony and of contact with Maori through the eyes of British colonists. These 'adventures' idealized some aspects of life in the colony and obviously, as autobiographies, put the authors at the centre of events. At the same time, the actual experience the writers had and their encounters with 'real life savages' continually fed the imaginations of people 'back home'. On the basis of these stories and the hard-sell of settlement companies, new migrants set off for their own adventures in the colonies armed with all their newly acquired misinformation about the availability of land, indigenous land, and the opportunity to make new lives. Those observers of indigenous peoples whose interest was of a more 'scientific' nature could be regarded as being far more dangerous in that they had theories to prove, evidence and data to gather and specific languages by which they could classify and describe the indigenous world. So, for example, skulls were measured and weighed to prove that 'primitive' minds were smaller than the European mind.[3]

As much as this is viewed as a problem within the fields of History and Anthropology, it is a similar issue that exists within charity. Our efforts can become Christian tourism when we visit those in other communities to confirm our beliefs that what we have to offer is much more valid than their lived experiences without really taking the time to get to know them. In philanthropy, we often make decisions without listening to those who are in those communities and base our donations and support on our perceptions of what we've read, been told, or our limited experiences.

If Christ is our example of leadership, then it is important that we note his qualities and characteristics in our approach. Christ was the ultimate servant leader. Servant leadership "begins with the natural feeling that one wants to serve, to serve first. Then conscious choice brings one to aspire to lead. That person is sharply different from one who is leader first . . . The difference manifests itself in the care taken by the servant-first to make sure that other people's highest priority needs are being served."[4]

Servant Leadership Model[5]

As a servant leader, it is not about advancing our agenda. Much like the Relational Cultural Theory model shared in the previous chapter, there are compliments in the Servant Leadership Model. Characteristics of Servant Leadership include:

- Listening
- Empathy
- Healing
- Awareness/Reflection
- Stewardship
- Interested in the growth and development of others
- Building community

Leadership is an important part of working in communities, but it is being aware of when it is time to lead and a time to serve. Most leaders are unaware of how their ideals of leadership can destroy projects and even lives. I think television has really warped our views of leadership. We believe it is all about wielding power over others. Expressions like "nice guys finish last" have informed our views about how we treat others, and successful leaders recognize that their greatest asset is the people we are blessed to lead. Ecclesiastes reminds us of the damage that domination has for everyone: "There is a time when a man lords it over others to his own hurt" (Ecclesiastes 8:9 NIV). Trust is key in building relationships. It can take years to build it and seconds to destroy it.

- Leaders build and maintain trust. Servant leaders recognize how their behavior impacts all.[6]

- Frequent dialogues exchange builds trust between leaders and followers. Servant leaders make relationships paramount.[7]

- The way the leader communicates impacts the follower's trust. Servant leaders understand the importance of creating safe spaces for communication to build trust.[8]

Leaders know that it is important to pay attention to not only what is spoken but the unspoken. So often we miss cues and take things out of context. Just as communication is important and key, we must be aware that there are multiple leadership styles and talents that exist in communities that are assets. Our job is to serve as a catalyst, creating space for individuals to flourish in their gifts. In 1983, Howard Gardner came up with a theory called Multiple Intelligences that challenged the idea that there was only one type of intelligence. Dr. Gardner listed eight bits of intelligence including interpersonal (people smart) and intrapersonal (self-smart). I believe that successful leaders must have the ability to self-reflect and know who they are as mentioned in chapter seventeen. It is also necessary that leaders understand the power of emotions in others and how this impacts their engagement. Daniel Goleman in 1995 wrote a book about emotional intelligence or EQ; the ability to manage and understand the power of emotions is just important as IQ. Emotional intelligence has four components: self-awareness, self-management, social awareness, and relationship management. All of these are a part of building relationships. Emotions are powerful. When we fail to recognize the feelings of those we are leading or working with, we can expect disconnection and a lack of transparency. Leaders also need to recognize that their opinions are not the only ones that matter. Another style of leadership, Adaptive Leadership, according to Heifetz et al. (2009), "builds a culture that values diverse views."[9] All of us must be flexible and willing to adjust as needed when working in communities especially when they are different than our own.

There are several leadership styles that are comparable to servant leadership worth noting. These styles can help us in making decisions and guide us in the way we engage with others in communities:

Relational Leadership is based on five components: process, inclusion, empowerment, purpose, and ethics.[10] Relational Leadership recognizes that in order to make things happen, we need people. It is about empowering others, helping them to not only see the purpose of the project but connect their purpose to it, and that we include others in an equitable and fair way.

Connective Leadership was coined by scholar Jean Lipman-Blumen who has conducted significant research on followership and toxic leadership. She defines Connective Leadership as "connecting individuals not only to their own tasks and ego drives, but also to those of the group and community that depend upon the accomplishment of mutual goals." It is leadership that connects individuals to others and others' goals, using a broad spectrum of behavioral strategies. It is leadership that "proceed(s) from a premise of connection. It shares responsibility, takes unthreatened pride in the accomplishments of colleagues and proteges, and experiences success without the compulsion to outdo others." Our goal is that those who live in communities feel empowered with the tools and resources they need to excel as we serve only in partnership and collaboration.[11]

Transformational Leadership is a "process that changes and transforms individuals."[12] Our goal in the community should not be that those who live in these areas are changed into our ideal of what they should look or be like. In the process of our interaction, our lives should be changed as well. If you are working in communities locally or even abroad as a part of a mission trip, and if you have not been changed in some way to better understand yourself, others, poverty, and the systems that impact the lives of others, you basically went on vacation. When I went to India as a part of a documentary in 2008, my life was radically changed. I saw individuals who were suffering from HIV, abandonment, and extreme poverty. I also witnessed hope and possibility through entrepreneurship programs for women and facilities built to provide care to those who were ill or orphaned. It was because of this experience that I became committed to working with women and building communities using partnerships as a tool. If that opportunity had not changed me for the better, I would have missed out on a chance to have my heartbroken. Bob Pearce, founder of

World Vision, stated, "Let the things that break God's heart, break mine."[13] My heart was broken, and my healing was through becoming a better person to assist in building God's kingdom on earth of love with others. How is God breaking your heart?

Authentic Leadership, according to the Center for Creative Leadership, is "the healthy alignment between internal values and beliefs and external behavior. Authenticity comes from finding your style and your way of leading—and making life decisions that reflect your values and your personality."[14] Authentic leaders understand that being honest about who you are isn't a license to say whatever you think without a filter or regard for the feelings of others. I've seen individuals in communities believe that because they are wealthy or older that it gives them the right to say whatever they want without regard to those who may be offended. They believe their wealth gives them permission to do and say whatever they want. I've seen others who believed that if they were helping in some way, this should also be a pass. Being authentic does not equate to being offensive. According to leadership scholar Peter Northouse,[15] authentic leaders have a sense of purpose which results in passion. These leaders have values that are not compromised and are committed to building relationships. They are disciplined, consistent, and have compassion.

All these complementary leadership styles can serve as a guide as we work in communities. At the core of each, relationships and trust are key. We are to steward relationships well. Regardless of the role, class, race, or any other category, we must place people at the center of what we do. "Leadership is always dependent on the context, but the context is established by the relationships we value."[16] We need to be aware of the historical and cultural context, but if we lose sight of the value of people, we are ineffective.

Narrative Change: Marginalized communities are not seeking a savior. That is what Jesus is for. They don't need to be rescued because leadership exists within those communities. Partner with them, and check your narrative on what you believe about those communities. Our job is to find ways to provide support, listen, and serve. Identify where God is at work and serve them. One of my favorite Bible studies is the book *Experiencing God: Knowing and Doing the Will of God* by Henry and Richard Blackaby and Claude King. According to the authors, God is always at work.[17] It's our job to use discernment and prayer to join Him. When working in communities, we must seek God and join the work that God is already a part of!

Call to Action: What is your leadership style when things are going well? When things are stressful? It is important to be aware of your leadership style especially when under stress. It's easy to be at our best when things are going well, but how do you handle difficult situations that challenge your way of thinking? How do you lead when there are disagreements? Leadership is about influence, and whatever you pay attention to your team will respond to it. If your focus is always on putting out fires and addressing the crisis, your team will focus on those things as well and possibly create an environment that feeds on being reactionary. How can you use your influence to make a difference and focus on what's important? How can you make sure that in all your interactions, you are centering people?

Scriptures to Ponder

Our leadership requires a willingness to serve first and foremost: "Yet it shall not be so among you; but whoever desires to become great among you, let him be your servant." (Matthew 20:26 NKJV)

Good leaders recognize the interest of others in making decisions: "Let nothing be done through selfish ambition or conceit, but in lowliness of mind let each esteem others better than himself. Let each of you look out not only for his own interests, but also for the interests of others." (Philippians 2:3-4 NKJV)

20

KNOW YOUR IMMUNITY TO CHANGE

Everyone thinks of changing the world, but no
one thinks of changing himself.

Leo Tolstoy

No matter our background, we all crave change. We want to see things
change in our families, in our jobs, in our relationships, in our government, and in our communities. Television, newspapers, and social
media daily remind us of the disparities, social and racial injustice, and
poverty in our country and our world. Change is something that we say we
want but if that is so true, why is it so difficult to make it happen? According to Robert Kegan and Lisa Lahey, authors of *Immunity to Change: How
to Overcome It and Unlock the Potential in Yourself and Your Organization*
state that "The problem is the inability to close the gap between what we
genuinely, even passionately, want and what we are actually able to do. Closing this gap is a central learning problem of the twenty-first century."[1] The
challenge is not the problem—it is our way of seeing and addressing the
problem. It is knowing the difference between issues that require adaptive
or technical solutions and quite often, we are applying the wrong solution
to a problem. Technical challenges are those that require a solution that
involves a skill. Adaptive challenges are those that skills cannot change and
require a change in ourselves and the way we view situations. Applying a
technical solution to an adaptive challenge does not solve a problem. Often,
our self-identity is a part of the adaptive challenge. "Adaptive challenges can
only be addressed through changes in people's priorities, beliefs, habits, and

loyalties."[2] If we really want to see a change in our communities, it begins with us. Many of us read a variety of books, listen to experts, and even attend conferences seeking content that will help, and yet, we leave excited and on fire only to go back to doing the exact same things we've been doing. Nothing changes. We have new information, but we are still doing the same thing.

When I was growing up, I remember hearing the expression that an old dog can't learn new tricks and yet, adult development theory has demonstrated that we can change contingent upon our mindsets. Our mindsets are instrumental to the way we see the world and how we engage with others. Kegan and Lahey list three mindsets that exist: the socialized, self-authoring, and self-transforming minds. No mindset is better than the other and the goal isn't to become one or the other. It is to become aware of it for ourselves and others so that we have the tools we need to change. Adults have different plateaus in mental complexity just as our communities have unique complexities. Maybe the reason we face some of the challenges is a direct correlation to our unwillingness to accept our differences and the unique complexities and identities that exist within us all.

Here are the mindsets. The socialized mind can be characterized by the following:

- Shaped by definitions and expectations of our environment

- Strongly influenced by what I think people want to hear

- Sensitive to and influenced by what it picks up

For example, when I was younger, I wanted to fit in. If my friends did not think something was interesting, I didn't necessarily agree, but I was quiet and failed to give my opinion. If I wanted to be accepted, I said what I thought would keep me off the radar and would limit attention toward me. If I heard something on the news that troubled me, I ran with it without further exploring another perspective because I was sensitive to what I heard. Although everyone doesn't do this, I think there are times in all our lives that we've had the socialized mindset.

The self-authoring mind does the following:

- Creates a filter for what it allows to come through

- Places priority on information that is sought to accomplish a plan

- If I didn't ask for the information and it is not relevant to me, it can't get through my filter.[3]

When I've been on Zoom calls for hours, I find that it is easy to listen only when I hear my name or words that register as important to me. Did that mean the information shared wasn't important? Not at all. I just wanted enough information that would get me closer to my goal.

The final mindset mentioned is self-transforming and has the following characteristics:

- Ability to look at a situation and also look through the situation

- Ability to see multiple systems at work at the same time

- Ability to see the positive and negative of a situation at the same time

In this mindset, it is the ability to do what Ronald Heifetz calls being on the balcony and the dance floor. "When you move back and forth between balcony and dance floor, you can continually assess what is happening in your organization and take corrective midcourse action."[4]

This not only applies to organizations but how we address issues in our lives and our communities. When we are self-transforming, we can get close to a situation and yet, step back from it to gain a clear, concise perspective in order to make a decision.

All these mindsets ultimately impact our ability to see the change we want in ourselves, in others, and in our communities. If we are easily influenced, the first time we experience disagreement, we will leave because it goes against what we believe. If we only want to hear what works for us, we fail to recognize the perspectives of others. Kegan and Lahey have created an Immunity Map that is a great tool to examine the reasons why we won't change. So often, it is because we have competing commitments that are at work when we say we want things to be different. This competing commitment previously served to protect us but is now preventing us from changing. For example, I wanted to lose weight, and even though I had the technical knowledge of what I needed to do, I had to really change my thinking about it. I realized after going through the process of completing an Immunity Map that each time I had tried to lose weight, something bad happened. When my father was dying of cancer, I was dieting. It was a dumb time to diet, but in my mind, I had started losing weight and I didn't want to stop. Afterward in my mind, I equated losing weight with my dad's death. Years later, I was training to participate in a half marathon, and once I was up to six miles, I got sick. Doctors could not figure out what was happening to my body. My mind combined losing weight with my father's death and those two experiences became blocks for me. Immediately, when I would begin to work out, I felt defeated. I felt like I was wasting my time. It wasn't until I realized this that I was able to take steps through small wins. I tested my big assumptions about my desire to lose weight, and when I realized that my way of thinking was impacting my ability to do what I knew I could do, those tiny steps moved into action. I haven't lost all the weight I want, but I am aware of how my thinking limited me in that situation.

The same thing happens in our communities. When we've had bad experiences or received incomplete information, we make decisions that are ill-advised. We must examine our true willingness for change beginning with ourselves.

Change is hard, and as we go through it, we cannot dismiss our thinking or our emotions. The Kübler-Ross Change Curve is a great explanation of what happens when we must deal with changes in our life but also think about what this looks like within a community: stages of the curve include shock and denial, anger, bargaining, depression, and acceptance, with one's energy levels falling and rising in step.[5] Communities also experience emotional changes when they have been promised so much only to be disappointed because the grant funding ran out or the agency changed its focus area and left them without the tools or resources to continue the work that was started. What a disservice this is to marginalized communities around the globe when people who claim to be committed leave only for another group to come in later and restart the process or change the priorities totally!

Over the next several years, the fallout from COVID-19 will require us to think differently about the way we see ourselves and one another. We will also need to think differently about communities. We will need to remove all stereotypes, biases, and discrimination that prevent true engagement to serve and collaborate. I strongly encourage you to read *Immunity to Change* by Kegan and Lahey. I have taken many individuals and groups through this process with great success. We need to really examine how we are in the midst of the change we so desperately claim that we want. We need to examine and explore our Immunity to Change in the areas of poverty in our country and world. We have the resources: the human, social and financial capital to do it. How can we bring these things together, leaving our egos aside, to really impact ALL of God's people? If we are honest, changing would require giving up a way of thinking that has served us well while neglecting others.

Narrative Change: Ronald Heifetz states, "People begin analyzing problems by personalizing them."[6] One thing that we cannot do in communities is comparing ourselves to others. Just because we were able to overcome poverty, illness, addiction, or other challenges does not mean that everyone can do the same thing. Empathy means I share and understand what you are going through. Yet, it is dangerous to think that others deal with trauma in the same way. Using tools like trauma-informed care can help us examine situations differently. Instead of looking at what's wrong with you, we must ask what happened to you.[7] Those experiences of trauma, compounded with race, class, gender, ability, and sexuality, shape us. For example, when I was a child, I mentioned we had to live with my uncle and aunt briefly due to a house fire. We were able to move back into our house months later. For someone else, they may have had a house fire as well. Because we had the same experience doesn't mean the variables were the same. We had support from our family. Some may not have relatives that are in a position to assist. We fail to think about the variables that may be far different in others and especially within communities. It is unfair when we label communities rooted in inaccurate thinking and perceptions based on our limited experiences. Although there may be similarities, we create standards for others that are not fair or equitable. Before we transform communities, change begins individually! What are your barriers to create the change needed in your home, your job, your church, and your community?

Despite the uncertainty we face, change is truly an opportunity. In the midst of uncertainty and ambiguity, God is at work: "See, I am doing a new thing! Now it springs up; do you not perceive it? I am making a way in the wilderness and streams in the wasteland" (Isaiah 43:19 NIV).

Call to Action: I struggle with severe allergies. I've been hospitalized with anaphylaxis three times in 2019. As my doctors tried to stop the effect of the reaction, we also needed to find out the trigger and cause. What was I encountering that made me so ill? In those moments, my body began to attack itself to try to eliminate the allergen. I think for many of us, our thinking does something similar. When we are faced with experiences that go against what we believe, we can create antibodies, that in the past may have served a purpose of protection, but at times, they turn against us, keeping us in a space that doesn't allow us to move forward. What in your life is keeping you from making the changes you need to be more engaged in your local area? What prevents you from being the neighbor that we are called to be (Luke 10:25-37)? What road have you traveled that made you ignore what you saw, and you chose to do nothing? Is there something you can do differently in the future?

FINAL REFLECTION

"Your corn is ripe today; mine will be so tomorrow. 'Tis profitable for us both, that I should labour with you today, and that you should aid me tomorrow. I have no kindness for you, and know you have as little for me. I will not, therefore, take any pains upon your account; and should I labour with you upon my own account, in expectation of a return, I know I should be disappointed, and that I should in vain depend upon your gratitude. Here then I leave you to labour alone; You treat me in the same manner. The seasons change; and both of us lose our harvests for want of mutual confidence and security."

David Hume

"Go to the People, Live with them, Love them, Learn from them, Work with them, Start with what they have, Build on what they know, and, in the end, when the work is done, the people will rejoice and they will say, 'We have done it ourselves.'"

Lao Tzu – China, 700 B.C.

For me, the ultimate goal is to make sure that relationships are paramount in everything we do. I often see the cross as an explanation of the power of relationships. The cross reaches up to God and out to people. When we don't keep those two in alignment and perspective, we miss out on the fullness of the abundant life we were designed to have. Our goal in communities is to make sure that it is not focused on ourselves, but it is centered around the people who live there. My prayer for you is that as you've read through this book you have been challenged, inspired, and filled with hope about what you can do to be a blessing to others. As you engage, especially in communities of color, and for Black people, be aware of triggering. Please know that the people you encounter every day, especially those who have different life experiences, face battles you are unaware of. How are you making sure that you are mindful of the triggers many of us face because of media and situations of injustice? Are you asking with sincerity how people are doing, checking in, and creating space not just for happiness and celebration but also for lament and tears?[1] In our desire to get things done, we realize the greatest resource we have is in people, and taking a break to refuel, listen, and pray is necessary. I hope that as we extend the grace we seek for ourselves to others, our world will change one relationship at a time.

Dr. Froswa' Booker-Drew

APPENDIX: REAL LIFE EXAMPLES

Real Life Example 1

I received this text message from a colleague one evening seeking counsel on a situation:

Anonymous: Hello how are you? Because I respect you and I know you will give me sound advice, I need to know to handle a situation when another nonprofit creates a press release to get credit for your event when they only made a donation. Our Thanksgiving distribution cost $125k, we received $30k from PG Foundation. They put out a press release (I found a copy). We have been doing this for the last three years, they got involved this year and now take full credit when they haven't done anything but cut a check and then they don't mention our organization or the city food pantry in the press release when we are doing all the leg work and it's our clients we are serving. I have no problem with them saying partnering but to do this is unacceptable. I just need to know what to say or not cause I'm pissed.

Me: I'm so sorry this is happening. It's frustrating and painful when you are doing the work and someone else takes the credit. As soon as possible, send a letter to the organization to restate the agreement you had regarding services provided. Moving forward, it's important to have a Memorandum of Agreement to ensure that all expectations are addressed. I also believe you should meet in person to discuss. You should also send out a press release on behalf of your organization to share the work with others the great work you are providing in the community. It's important for you and your organization to control your narrative despite what they might say or do. Continue the great work you are doing. Please make sure you are documenting through email and written agreements all of your conversations that include discussions on how media will be handled, expectations for the partnership, and other important issues with any agency to avoid this as much as possible in the future.

Narrative Change: Although well intentioned to help, foundations and large nonprofits do not realize that in their desire to promote the goodness they are a part of, they frequently minimize the work of smaller organizations often led by people of color. In taking credit for the work, they are disingenuous. The larger organizations gain visibility for the work being conducted, which leads to more opportunities without consideration for the organization that is carrying the load.

Thoughts to Consider: As much as we talk about the importance of equity, the nonprofit community must begin to evaluate the exploitation of communities of color in taking credit for the work and using the guise of collaboration to appear as the savior and hero in the end.

- Are there ways to make sure that marginalized organizations that you support financially are also given visibility through your network instead of only highlighting your contribution?

- If you are a part of an organization or foundation that supports smaller nonprofits, is there an opportunity to create joint press releases or direct funding to those organizations?

Real Life Example 2

Executive Director: So glad that several board members were able to visit the homes we recently built in X community. This area is one that has been impoverished for generations and we are glad that we could help these families have a place to call home. Through your efforts and donations, we've been able to help several families have a home.

Board Member: When we build homes in the future, we need to make sure these individuals actually need it. I saw old model luxury cars in the driveway and that is a problem.

Narrative Change: The board member's comment reflects what many believe. If we are helping someone, they should not have access to anything nice. If they have access, they do not need any help. This isn't true. Remembering the Good Samaritan story (Luke 10:25-37), the Samaritan didn't say, "He needs to stay outside because he has no money." "He is less than me and so he doesn't deserve what I have. He needs to work for it." The board member made an assumption. He had no idea how the person may have received the car—it was a donation, passed down from a relative, something that they had before they lost everything. It isn't our job to judge—allow God to do that.

> "Judge not, that you be not judged. For with the judgment, you pro-nounce you will be judged, and with the measure you use it will be measured to you. Why do you see the speck that is in your brother's eye, but do not notice the log that is in your own eye? Or how can you say to your brother, 'Let me take the speck out of your eye,' when there is the log in your own eye? You hypocrite, first take the log out of your own eye, and then you will see clearly to take the speck out of your brother's eye." (Matthew 7:1-5 ESV)

We are to be good stewards but how dare we believe that we do not receive gifts that we did not deserve. We have received favor from individuals in our life that we didn't deserve. I've been given gifts by others that I didn't work for. The ultimate gift we have all received that we did not deserve was eternal life. "For God so loved the world, that he gave his only Son, that whoever believes in him should not perish but have eternal life" (John 3:16 ESV). Just as God has blessed us with the best gift ever and we did not deserve it, it is arrogant to believe that we can now play judge over the lives of others. All of these things are God's resources. God is in control.

Thoughts to Consider: Have there been times that you have been judgmental toward others based on the outer appearance? Maybe we noticed a luxury car or a designer purse that belonged to someone that we felt didn't deserve it? How did you respond? Did you feel as if they did not deserve it? Why? Where does this feeling that someone does or does not deserve come from?

There is a term in psychology called the shadow self. "The 'shadow' is the side of your personality that contains all the parts of yourself that you don't want to admit to having."[1] It is important to know this side of who you are and why you think or believe the way you do. Otherwise, it manifests in the way we deal with and treat others. It shows up in our generosity and who we deem valuable enough to receive support. Pay attention to this. You could miss out on so many opportunities not to transform others be to be trans-formed. Even though this is how we have been conditioned, we must change this. "Do not conform to the pattern of this world, but be transformed by the renewing of your mind. Then you will be able to test and approve what God's will is—his good, pleasing and perfect will" (Romans 12:2 NIV).

Real Life Example 3

Anonymous: I'm too busy to give my time. I have so much to do with my work, my family, and there is such little time left in the day that I don't know how I can serve. If I don't work and take care of these other obligations, I can't take care of those things that are important.

Narrative Change: Many of us feel as if we have so much to do. I'll never forget meeting a lady several years ago who told me I was in captivity to activity. Wow! We are doing so much but it isn't necessarily getting us closer to our goals and we definitely do not have enough time to sow into the lives of others. There is a concept called "time poverty" which is the belief that as we do not have enough money, we feel as if we do not have enough time. "When economies grow and incomes rise, everyone's time becomes more valuable. And the more valuable something becomes, the scarcer it seems. When people see their time in terms of money, they often grow stingy with the former to maximise the latter."[2]

In essence, we equate time to money and when we are doing things that do not provide an immediate reward, we don't see the value in it. There is a danger in "time poverty." According to one, "Most people today report feeling persistently 'time poor'—like they have too many things to do and not enough time to do them. This is critical because time poverty is linked to lower well-being, physical health, and productivity."[3]

There are many benefits to being generous, enough that your very life depends upon it. Generosity does the following:

It lowers:

- Blood Pressure
- Risk of Dementia
- Anxiety
- Depression
- Cardiovascular issues[4]

Researchers at Notre Dame studied two thousand individuals in one of the most comprehensive studies on generosity. They found that "Americans who are very giving in relationships—being emotionally available and hospitable—are much more likely to be in excellent health (48 percent) than those who are not (31 percent)."[5] When we are not generous and mistreat others, it actually increases our stress levels.[6]

Assisting others and giving of your time even increases your longevity. Another study "found that volunteerism reduced mortality rates more than exercising four times weekly and attending church regularly (another behavior tied to improved mental health and greater longevity)."[7]

We must recognize the value of giving and making it a part of our schedule. It not only provides health benefits, but our lives are enriched as a result of it. So, give consistently and, while you are at it, go to church too!

Real Life Example 4

A board was interviewing candidates for a CEO role. The role was interim with the possibility of full-time employment but no benefits.

With applicants of various backgrounds, the board recognized that the search may prevent BIPOCs from participating due to the length of the role as well as the lack of benefits. For many of the White candidates, the ability to take a role with these limitations was not problematic because of various supports they had in place. For many of the candidates of color, these issues were barriers.

Narrative Change: It's important that in our hiring practices, we pay attention to issues that may prevent people of color from accepting opportunities including examining our ideas of leadership. Quite often, we seek charismatic leaders that "fit" our image of leadership—attractive, fit, well spoken, and visionary. What happens when candidates apply who have the skills we need but because they do not look the way we want, we exclude them from moving forward in the search? We deny individuals that could provide unique experiences and perspectives, along with the credentials we need that could take us to another level, but our preconceived ideas may limit us and them. In doing this, we all lose.

Call to Action: How can your organization examine its biases and internal protocols that could create barriers for diversity to flourish? What does this look like in your church? Are you creating a space that is welcoming and addresses the issues that impact the diverse populations you seek to include? In the age of social unrest and COVID-19, many Black members who attend multicultural congregations are leaving. Pastors failed to correlate the impact of COVID-19 on the Black community and some even taunted congregants for not attending in person. Other congregations remained silent on issues that impacted the Black community while continuing services every Sunday not recognizing the pain many of those they claimed to love suffered. I would encourage you to read the following articles:

- "A Quiet Exodus: Why Black Worshipers Are Leaving White Evangelical Churches," March 9, 2018[8]

- "What to Do about Blacks Leaving White Churches," May 17, 2018[9]

- "As a Black Person, I'm Done Helping White Christians Feel Better about Race," July 13, 2020[10]

- "The Church's Black Exodus," October 11, 2020[11]

As the church is also a significant philanthropic resource in our country, it is imperative that we also begin to address the impact it has had on giving and its issues with race. Although there have been numerous books written about race and the church, I would be remiss not to at least bring up the issue and encourage the church community to begin to explore its own past and present in addressing racism and systemic injustice through its giving practices. This book is not comprehensive in its discussion of the church but was written for faith-based nonprofits often connected to churches and individuals who work or volunteer in the nonprofit sector and identify as Christian.

Real Life Example 5

"Brandon," a Black man, was hired at an organization located in his community to provide strategy. The organization has been in existence for several years with a track record of serving those impacted by incarceration combined with substance abuse issues. Its board is primarily White and so is the senior leadership. This organization started as a ministry and, despite its growth, it has failed to develop its infrastructure. Brandon noticed that the organization has not set expected outcomes and that as much as he tried to stress the importance of having these metrics, the board and some of the individual donors ignored his warning. They continued doing things as usual and saw those served as "the helped," with no real desire to move the mindset from ministry to a business. The organization's marketing always displays its Black and Brown clients to show more of their "brokenness" instead of their "breakthroughs" and success. This organization does not partner with other organizations in the community but seeks to work only with other organizations outside of the area, leaving indigenous leaders out of the decision-making. Ultimately, Brandon realized that he was hired to serve as a face of the organization without real power to make changes.

Narrative Change: So often, ministries traditionally led and founded by White leadership in communities of color that become nonprofits do not consider the impact of their decisions. They hire Black faces in nonprofit and ministry spaces without ceding the power to make changes and decisions. The leader checks a box to prove a point about diversity without actual changes in the ethos and operation of the organization to be inclusive. At best, these organizations are tolerant—who wants to be tolerated? At their worst, they are condescending, divisive, secretive, and demoralizing. They see those that are served as needing "help" without recognizing the systems and structures that contribute to this person's need. This is never acknowledged which leads to the belief that everything depends on the personal responsibility of the client rather than a collective responsibility. This can not only impact the way individuals are viewed but also the implementation and delivery of services.

These organizations do not partner well with other organizations in the local communities, which are often led by people of color. Several of these organizations I've encountered often see their involvement with local leaders and organizations as an afterthought. The belief cannot be that these organizations aren't working and that your presence will serve as the solution. These organizations often do not have the access to networks of influence or money, which can be limiting but does not negate the impact of the work.

Call to Action: How does your organization address cultural differences and dynamics? How does your organization evaluate leadership and organizational culture to ensure that it is a place truly welcoming for Black and Brown senior leaders to thrive? Has your organization completed a racial equity audit to examine possible barriers internally and externally? Is training on racial equity conducted consistently, and how do you monitor progress? What does success look like?

Real Life Example 6

As evacuees moved to Dallas from New Orleans due to Hurricane Ida, hearts were compelled to do something. For many, it was serving food, and for others, it was donating money and clothing. Several Pastors commented that many of the donations of clothing and furniture were not usable. One remarked, "If it was trash in North Dallas, it'll be trash in South Dallas, but I guess they don't think we deserve better." Donating useless items takes time away to minister and deal with issues due to the time absorbed by going through and sorting items. Many organizations report that they end up with more trash which creates not only a time challenge but a resource issue to remove them.

Narrative Change: The belief that those who are struggling financially would be happy with anything continues to affirm thinking that poor people should be appreciative of whatever they receive. The adage "Beggars can't be choosers" is rooted in entitlement. The Bible is very clear about this: "Do to others as you would like them to do to you" (Luke 6:31). Would you want someone to give you clothing that has holes in it or visible sweat stains?

Could you have dignity and pride knowing that another person thought so low of you that they would give you used underwear? If it isn't something you would give to your relatives or friends, why would you feel comfortable in giving it to a stranger (or, seen biblically, your neighbor)? The way we donate items to others has to be changed.

Call to Action: Is there an opportunity to evaluate your giving personally as it relates to used items like clothing, furniture, and appliances? What is the litmus test that is used to determine if items need to be tossed? Does your church have a policy in place for donating used items and the disposal of those items before being donated?

NOTES

Introduction

1   Prejean 2021.
2   For more information on these definitions and why they are important, visit https://www.healthline.com/health/bipoc-meaning.

1   Myth: Poor People Are Lazy

1   O'Reilly 2007.
2   Desmond 2018.
3   Wetzel and Ward 2020,
4   Bacon, Lee, Weber, and Duran 2020.
5   Zauzmer 2019.
6   Pew Research Center 2020b.
7   Pew Research Center 2020a.
8   Prince n.d.
9   Interview on Bill Bennett's *Morning in America Show*, 2014, https://www.youtube.com/watch?v=PLF61QctgqU.
10   Race Forward 2021.
11   Poverty USA 2019.
12   American Economic Association 2019.
13   Kneebone and Holmes 2016.
14   Infórmate DFW 2020.
15   Edwards 2021.
16   https://inlandport.org/.
17   FDIC 2017.
18   FDIC 2017.

19   Hartline-Grafton 2017.
20   USDA ERS 2021.
21   Children's Defense Fund 2020.
22   Trauma-Informed Care Implementation Resource Center, "What Is Trauma-Informed Care?" accessed August 19, 2021, https://www.traumainformedcare.chcs.org/what-is-trauma-informed-care/.
23   Myers 2020.

2   Myth: A College Degree and a Job Will Solve Poverty

1   Tyko 2019.
2   Nova 2019.
3   Shinneman 2019.
4   Statistical Atlas 2018.
5   https://www.texas-demographics.com/75215-demographics.
6   Haveman and Wolff 2004.
7   U.S. Bureau of Labor Statistics 2019.
8   Berman 2018.
9   Feeding America n.d.
10   O'Brien 2020.
11   https://www.score.org.
12   https://usa.generation.org.
13   https://www.yearup.org.
14   https://educationalequity.org/.
15   https://leadershipisd.org/.
16   To learn more about advocacy organizations addressing student loans and financial aid, visit https://www.finaid.org/.

3   Myth: Homeless People Like Being Homeless

1   Dam 2019.
2   Dam 2019.
3   Reynolds 2014.
4   Young 2001.
5   Dam 2019.
6   Murray and Hampton 2021.
7   HUD 2019.
8   addictioncenter.com.
9   Tozier 2019.
10   National Alliance to End Homelessness 2021.
11   Linkins, Brya, and Chandler 2008.

12 Green Doors n.d.
13 The Times Editorial Board 2018.
14 McNulty 2019.

4 Myth: Welfare Is the Problem

1 Interview on race and IQ, "Think Tank with Ben Wattenberg," PBS, 1994, https://www.pbs.org/thinktank/transcript129.html.
2 Murray 2000.
3 Center on Budget and Policy Priorities n.d.
4 Meyer and Floyd 2020.
5 Gaiter 2016.
6 Kaiser Family Foundation 2021.
7 Jacobs, Perry, and MacGillvary 2015.
8 Benjamin Franklin Historical Society 2014.
9 Tucker, Edwards, Foley, and Diani 2002.
10 de Tocqueville 2000.

5 Myth: Following the Rules Ensures Success

1 Cáccamo 1998.
2 Harris 2019.
3 Stephens 2020.
4 Harris 2019.

6 Myth: Black, Single, Teen Mothers Perpetuate Poverty

1 Cosby 2004.
2 Office of Population Affairs n.d.
3 Martin, Hamilton, Osterman, and Driscoll 2021.
4 http://www.violashouse.org/.
5 https://www.lullabyhouses.org/about.
6 https://www.ilooklikelove.org/.
7 https://bridgescanhelp.org/.
8 https://cartershouse.org/.

7 Myth: Black Fathers Are Absentee Dads

1 Jones and Mosher 2013.
2 The Sentencing Project 2018.
3 NewsRadio 1080 KRLD, "Fatal Wrong Way Crash Suspect Charged with Two Counts of Murder," 2019, https://krld.radio.com/articles/fatal-wrong-way-crash-suspect-charged-two-counts-murder.

4   Myers 2019.
5   Murphey and Cooper 2015.
6   Moorer 2019; Beckner, Toon, Chammah, and Barajas 2019.
7   Youth.gov n.d.
8   Murphey and Cooper 2015.

8   Myth: BIPOCs Do Not Give

1   Reid 2019.
2   Understand Together n.d.
3   https://www.blackbenefactors.org/.
4   https://blackswanacademy.org/.
5   https://www.scholarchipsfund.org/.
6   https://thewomensfoundation.org/african-american-womens-giving -circle/.
7   http://www.blackphilanthropymonth.com/.
8   https://www.contradictionsoffairhope.com/.
9   VoyageDallas 2017.
10   https://www.txwf.org/heritage-giving-fund/.
11   Ashley and James 2018.
12   https://moorephilanthropy.com/.
13   https://philanthropytogether.org/.

9   Myth: BIPOCs Do Not Have a History of Giving

1   Vaid and Maxton 2017, 10.
2   Vaid and Maxton 2017, 11.
3   Women's Philanthropy Institute 2019, 9.
4   http://www.blackgreek.com/divinenine/.
5   Women's Philanthropy Institute 2019, 4.
6   Pilgrim 2004.
7   Clark 2018.

10   Myth: White Wealth Is Not Built on Slavery

1   Horowitz, Brown, and Cox 2019.
2   Ross 2019.
3   Sacerdote 2002.
4   Lee 2019.
5   Somin 2015.
6   Wigglesworth 2012.
7   Vaughn 2020; Worth 2020.
8   Villarosa 2019.

9   Villarosa 2019.
10 Hoffman, Trawalter, Axt, and Oliver 2016.
11 Eligon 2020.
12 Siefker n.d.
13 https://bigtex.com/supporting-texans/education/.
14 Hains 2019.
15 Lumen Learning n.d.

11 Myth: BIPOCs Are Unavailable to Serve and Lead

1   Black Indy Live Staff 2019.
2   *The Journal of Blacks in Higher Education* 2018.
3   The Kirwin Institute 2012.
4   The Kirwin Institute 2012.
5   Levine 2019.
6   Daniel 2019.
7   Bourke and Titus 2020.
8   The website http://racialequitytools.org/ has so many resources includ-
    ing templates that can serve as a reference. There are also several
    thought leaders in this space that you should consider following. You
    can check them out at https://www.forbes.com/sites/janicegassam/
    2019/11/02/10-diversity-and-inclusion-trailblazers-you-need-to-get
    -familiar-with/ and definitely follow Janice Gassam, who consistently
    writes about this topic.

12 Leveraging Social Capital for Connections

1   Putnam 2000, 19.
2   Putnam 2000, 11–13.
3   Zacharakis and Flora 2005.
4   Ritter 2020.
5   Terrion 2006.
6   Tilly 1998.
7   Onyx, Edwards, and Bullen 2007.
8   Schön 1991.
9   Morin 2021.
10 Schön 1987.

13 Flourishing and the Increase of Other Forms of Capital

1   Da Graca and Dougherty 2015.
2   Edwards 2020.

3   Edwards 2020.
4   Neitzel 2020.
5   Yosso 2005, 70
6   Dominguez and Watkins 2003.
7   Figure based on Tara J. Yosso, "Whose Culture Has Capital?" (Yosso 2005). Yosso's figure was adapted from Melvin L. Oliver and Thomas M. Shapiro, *Black Wealth/White Wealth: A New Perspective on Racial Inequality* (Oliver and Shapiro 1995).

14   Knowing Your Community and Asset Mapping

1   West 2017.
2   Mathie and Cunningham 2002, 6.
3   Daniel 2019.
4   Jaramillo 2017.
5   Figure created by the author and Baylor University Press.

15   Weaving Networks Actually Works

1   http://networkweaver.blogspot.com/2010/04/what-is-network-weaver.html#.
2   Kennedy and Chandler 2019, 3.
3   https://www.worldvision.org/our-work/country-profiles/united-states.
4   https://networkweaver.com/.
5   Figure created by the author and Baylor University Press.

16   Analyzing Systems and the Post-COVID-19 Impact

1   Thomas-Breitfeld 2017.
2   Thomas-Breitfeld and Kunreuther 2019.
3   Goodman 2016.
4   Badger 2017.
5   Bertrand and Mullainathan 2003.
6   Schott Foundation 2012.
7   Schott Foundation 2012.
8   NAACP 2021.
9   Perrin and Turner 2019; Fishbane and Tomer 2020.
10   Dorn, Hancock, Sarakatsannis, and Viruleg 2020.
11   Mental Health America n.d.
12   https://www.beam.community/whatwebelieve.
13   https://thelovelandfoundation.org/loveland-therapy-fund/.

14 Highberger 2020.
15 Ollove and Vestal 2020.

17 Recognizing the Role of Power Dynamics

1 https://www.arteachingcollective.com/positionality.html.
2 Illustration from Joanna Simpson, *Everyone Belongs: A Toolkit for Applying Intersectionality* (Simpson 2009).
3 Smooth 2013.

18 Living Lives of Empathy

1 Walker and Rosen 2004, 4.
2 Jordan and Baker 2008, 2.
3 Jordan, Hartling, and Walker 2004, 35.
4 Jordan 2000, 32.
5 Illustration from the personal blog of Tom Graves/Tetradian (Graves 2014).
6 Cherry 2020.
7 Schön 1987.
8 https://narrative4.com/.

19 Leading (and Following) Is Critical in Relationships

1 Booker-Drew 2014.
2 Portman and Garrett 2005, 289.
3 Smith 2012, 82.
4 Greenleaf 1977, 27.
5 Figure based on illustrations in chapter 4, "Explaining the Servant Mindset: The OLA Servant Leadership Model," in James Laub, *Leveraging the Power of Servant Leadership* (Laub 2018).
6 Depree 2006; https://sites.psu.edu/leadership/2013/03/31/servant-leadership-in-the-modern-workplace/.
7 Errol and Winston 2005.
8 Errol and Winston 2005.
9 Heifetz, Linsky, and Grashow 2009, 16.
10 Carifio 2010.
11 Lipman-Blumen 1992.
12 Northouse 2019.
13 Stearn 2018.
14 Leading Effectively Staff 2020.

15   Northouse 2019.
16   Wheatley 1992, 144.
17   Blackaby, Blackaby, and King 2008.

20   Know Your Immunity to Change

1   Kegan and Lahey 2009, 2.
2   Heifetz, Linsky, and Grashow 2009.
3   Booker-Drew 2013.
4   Heifetz, Linsky, and Grashow 2009, 8.
5   For a complete explanation and diagram of the change curve, see
     Kübler-Ross 1969.
6   Heifetz, Linsky, and Grashow 2009, 2.
7   Trauma-Informed Care Implementation and Resource Center n.d.

Final Reflection

1   Booker-Drew 2021.

Appendix

1   Blundell 2017.
2   *The Economist* 2014.
3   Giurge and Whillans 2020, 2.
4   Stat 2015.
5   Smith 2014.
6   Queensland University of Technology 2014.
7   Renter 2015.
8   Robertson 2018.
9   Seales 2018.
10   Stewart 2020.
11   Mathis 2020.

Glossary of Terms

1   Schwartz 2019.
2   Collaborative for Neighborhood Transformation n.d.
3   https://www.vistacampus.gov/what-asset-mapping.
4   https://en.wikipedia.org/wiki/Asset_poverty.
5   *Psychology Today* n.d.
6   https://www.merriam-webster.com/dictionary/BIPOC.
7   DurhamCares 2017; https://ccda.org/about/philosophy/.
8   https://en.wikipedia.org/wiki/Class_discrimination.

9   Understand Together n.d.

10   http://people.tamu.edu/~i-choudhury/culture.html.

11   Brondolo, Mays, Jackson, and Jones 2019.

12   Picardo 2020.

13   https://en.wikipedia.org/wiki/Identity_(social_science).

14   YW Boston 2017.

15   Kruse 2013.

16   McAdams 2011.

17   Jensen 2009, chapter preview at http://www.ascd.org/publications/
      books/109074/chapters/Understanding-the-Nature-of-Poverty.aspx.

18   https://dictionary.cambridge.org/us/dictionary/english/prejudice.

19   https://www.dictionary.com/browse/privilege. To learn more about
      White privilege, see Greenberg 2017.

20   https://www.merriam-webster.com/dictionary/racism.

21   https://en.wikipedia.org/wiki/Sexism.

22   Aspen Institute n.d.

23   ACEs Aware n.d.

GLOSSARY OF TERMS

Although not all of these terms are in the book, I would encourage you to review them to learn more about how they exist and show up for you in your life personally and professionally.

Antiracist—Ibram X. Kendi defines an antiracist "as someone who is expressing an antiracist idea or supporting an antiracist policy with their actions. To be antiracist is to think nothing is behaviorally wrong or right—inferior or superior—with any of the racial groups. Whenever the antiracist sees individuals behaving positively or negatively, the antiracist sees exactly that: individuals behaving positively or negatively, not representatives of whole races. To be antiracist is to deracialize behavior, to remove the tattooed stereotype from every racialized body. Behavior is something humans do, not races do."[1]

Asset-Based Community Development—"ABCD builds on the assets that are already found in the community and mobilizes individuals, associations, and institutions to come together to build on their assets—not concentrate on their needs."[2]

Asset Mapping—"A tool that relies on a core belief of asset-based community development; namely, that good things exist in communities and that those things can be highlighted and encouraged—these are assets suited to advancing those communities. Asset Mapping is a means, not an end."[3]

Asset Poverty—"An economic and social condition that is more persistent and prevalent than income poverty. It is a household's inability to access wealth resources that are sufficient to provide for basic needs for a period of three months. Basic needs refer to the minimum standards for consumption and acceptable needs."[4]

Bias—"A tendency, inclination, or prejudice toward or against something or someone. Some biases are positive and helpful—like choosing to only eat foods that are considered healthy or staying away from someone who has knowingly caused harm. But biases are often based on stereotypes, rather than actual knowledge of an individual or circumstance. Whether positive or negative, such cognitive shortcuts can result in prejudgments that lead to rash decisions or discriminatory practices."[5]

BIPOC—"Black, Indigenous, (and) People of Color. POC is widely used as an umbrella term for all people of color, but now a different acronym is suddenly gaining traction on the internet—BIPOC, which stands for Black, Indigenous, People of Color. People are using the term to acknowledge that not all people of color face equal levels of injustice. They say BIPOC is significant in recognizing that Black and Indigenous people are severely impacted by systemic racial injustices."[6]

Christian Community Development—"The eight key components of Christian Community Development (CCD) make up a ministry philosophy birthed out of decades of work to address systemic poverty and injustice from within communities that have been marginalized. Formulated from the life and work of John Perkins, The Christian Community Development Association began decades ago and is a network of people, organizations, and congregations who have modeled their work off the eight key components. The CCDA Philosophy page offers a helpful overview and description of each of the eight components:

- Relocation
- Reconciliation
- Redistribution
- Listening to the Community
- Leadership Development
- Empowerment
- Church-Based
- Wholistic"[7]

Classism—"Class discrimination, also known as classism, is prejudice or discrimination on the basis of social class. It includes individual attitudes, behaviors, systems of policies and practices that are set up to benefit the upper class at the expense of the lower class. Social class refers to the group-

ing of individuals in a hierarchy based on wealth, income, education, occu-
pation, and social network."[8]

Community Assets—"The collective resources which individuals and communities have at their disposal; those which can be leveraged to develop effective
solutions to promote social inclusion and improve the health and well-being
of citizens. Assets include organisations, associations and individuals."[9]

Culture—"Refers to the knowledge, experience, beliefs, values, attitudes, mean-
ings, hierarchies, religion, notions of time, roles, spatial relations, concepts
of the universe, and material objects and possessions acquired by a group of
people in the course of generations through individual and group striving.
Culture is the knowledge shared by a group of people. Culture is communication, communication is culture. A culture is a way of life of a group of
people—the behaviors, beliefs, values, and symbols that they accept, generally without thinking about them, and that are passed along by communication and imitation from one generation to the next. Culture is a collective
programming of the mind that distinguishes the members of one group or
category of people from another."[10]

Discrimination—"The unfair or prejudicial treatment of people and groups
based on characteristics such as race, gender, age or sexual orientation."[11]

Gentrification—"The transformation of a city neighborhood from low value to
high value. Gentrification is also viewed as a process of urban development
in which a neighborhood or portion of a city develops rapidly in a short
period of time, often as a result of urban-renewal programs. This process is
often marked by inflated home prices and displacement of a neighborhood's
previous residents."[12]

Giving Circle—According to the Forum of Regional Associations of Grantmakers' More Giving Together, a giving circle "is formed when individuals come
together and pool their dollars, decide together where to give the money
(and other resources such as volunteer time), and learn together about their
community and philanthropy."

Identity—"The qualities, beliefs, personality, looks or expressions that make a
person or group."[13]

Intersectionality—"A framework for conceptualizing a person, group of people,
or social problem as affected by a number of discriminations and disadvantages. It takes into account people's overlapping identities and experiences in
order to understand the complexity of prejudices they face. In other words,
intersectional theory asserts that people are often disadvantaged by multiple
sources of oppression: their race, class, gender identity, sexual orientation,

religion, and other identity markers. Intersectionality recognizes that identity markers (e.g. 'woman' and 'black') do not exist independently of each other, and that each informs the others, often creating a complex convergence of oppression."[14]

Leadership—According to Kevin Kruse, "Leadership is a process of social influence, which maximizes the efforts of others, towards the achievement of a goal."[15]

Narrative Identity—"The internalized and evolving story of the self that a person constructs to make sense and meaning out of his or her life."[16]

Poverty (types)—

- "**Situational poverty** is generally caused by a sudden crisis or loss and is often temporary. Events causing situational poverty include environmental disasters, divorce, or severe health problems.

- **Generational poverty** occurs in families where at least two generations have been born into poverty. Families living in this type of poverty are not equipped with the tools to move out of their situations.

- **Absolute poverty,** which is rare in the United States, involves a scarcity of such necessities as shelter, running water, and food. Families who live in absolute poverty tend to focus on day-to-day survival.

- **Relative poverty** refers to the economic status of a family whose income is insufficient to meet its society's average standard of living.

- **Urban poverty** occurs in metropolitan areas with populations of at least 50,000 people. The urban poor deal with a complex aggregate of chronic and acute stressors (including crowding, violence, and noise) and are dependent on often-inadequate large-city services.

- **Rural poverty** occurs in nonmetropolitan areas with populations below 50,000. In rural areas, there are more single-guardian households, and families often have less access to services, support for disabilities, and quality education opportunities. Programs to encourage transition from welfare to work are problematic in remote rural areas, where job opportunities are few (Whitener, Gibbs, & Kusmin, 2003). The rural poverty rate is growing and has exceeded the urban rate every year since data collection began in the 1960s. The difference between the two poverty rates has averaged about 5 percent for the last 30 years, with urban rates near 10–15 percent and rural rates near 15–20 percent (Jolliffe, 2004)."[17]

Prejudice—"An unfair and unreasonable opinion or feeling, especially when formed without enough thought or knowledge."[18]

Privilege—"A right, immunity, or benefit enjoyed by a particular person or a restricted group of people beyond the advantages of most."[19]

Racism—"A belief that race is a fundamental determinant of human traits and capacities and that racial differences produce an inherent superiority of a particular race; the systemic oppression of a racial group to the social, economic, and political advantage of another; a political or social system founded on racism and designed to execute its principles."[20]

Sexism—"Prejudice or discrimination based on one's sex or gender. Sexism can affect anyone, but it primarily affects women and girls. It has been linked to stereotypes and gender roles and may include the belief that one sex or gender is intrinsically superior to another."[21]

Social Capital—The networks of relationships among people who live and work in a particular society, enabling that society to function effectively.

Social Networks—A group of individuals connected by interpersonal relationships. Also can refer to social media platforms.

Systemic or Structural Racism—A system in which public policies, institutional practices, cultural representations, and other norms work in various, often reinforcing ways to perpetuate racial group inequity. It identifies dimensions of our history and culture that have allowed privileges associated with "whiteness" and disadvantages associated with "color" to endure and adapt over time. Structural racism is not something that a few people or institutions choose to practice. Instead it has been a feature of the social, economic and political systems in which we all exist.[22]

Trauma Informed Care—"Trauma-informed care recognizes and responds to the signs, symptoms, and risks of trauma to better support the health needs of patients who have experienced Adverse Childhood Experiences (ACEs) and toxic stress.

Trauma-informed care is a framework that involves:

- Understanding the prevalence of trauma and adversity and their impacts on health and behavior;

- Recognizing the effects of trauma and adversity on health and behavior;

- Training leadership, providers, and staff on responding to patients with best practices in trauma-informed care;

- Integrating knowledge about trauma and adversity into policies, procedures, practices and treatment planning; and

- Avoiding re-traumatization by approaching patients who have experienced ACEs or other adversities with non-judgmental support."[23]

REFERENCES

ACEs Aware. N.d. "Trauma-Informed Care: Understanding and Caring for Patients Affected by Toxic Stress." Accessed July 26, 2021. https://www .acesaware.org/ace-fundamentals/principles-of-trauma-informed-care/.

Addiction Center. 2021. "Hallucinogens and History." *Recovery Worldwide* (podcast). https://www.addictioncenter.com/community/episode -23-hallucinogens-and-history/.

American Economic Association. 2019. "The Unequal Burden of a Gasoline Tax." https://www.aeaweb.org/research/charts/second-best-gasoline -tax-burden#:~:text=The%20figure%20actually%20hides%20a,their%20 income%20in%20gasoline%20taxes.

Ashley, S., and J. James. February 28, 2018. "Despite the Racial Wealth Gap, Black Philanthropy Is Strong." Urban Institute. https://www.urban.org/ urban-wire/despite-racial-wealth-gap-black-philanthropy-strong.

Aspen Institute. N.d. "Glossary for Understanding the Dismantling Structural Racism/Promoting Racial Equity Analysis." https://www.aspeninstitute .org/wp-content/uploads/files/content/docs/rcc/RCC-Structural-Racism -Glossary.pdf.

Bacon, L., G. Lee, J. Weber, and L. A. Duran. 2020. *Laying the Groundwork: How States Can Improve Access to Continued Education to People in the Criminal Justice System.* New York: CSG Justice Center. https:// csgjusticecenter.org/publications/laying-the-groundwork/.

Badger, E. 2017. "Whites Have Huge Wealth Edge over Blacks (but Don't Know It)." *New York Times.* https://www.nytimes.com/interactive/2017/ 09/18/upshot/black-white-wealth-gap-perceptions.html.

Beckner, A., J. Toon, M. Chammah, and M. Barajas. 2019. "Why I Started a Book Club in the Harris County Jail." *Texas Observer*. https://www.texasobserver.org/why-i-started-a-book-club-in-the-harris-county-jail/.

Benjamin Franklin Historical Society. 2014. "Junto Club." http://www.benjamin-franklin-history.org/junto-club/.

Berman, J. 2018. "There Are 3.6 Million College Graduates Living in Poverty." MarketWatch. https://www.marketwatch.com/story/there-are-36-million-college-graduates-living-in-poverty-2018-09-12.

Bertrand, M., and S. Mullainathan. 2003. "Are Emily and Greg More Employable Than Lakisha and Jamal? A Field Experiment on Labor Market Discrimination." NBER. https://www.nber.org/papers/w9873.

Black Indy Live Staff. 2019. "Purdue President Mitch Daniels Calls African American Students 'Creatures', Faces Backlash." https://www.blackindylive.com/purdue-president-mitch-daniels-calls-african-american-students-creatures-faces-backlash/.

Blackaby, H. T., R. Blackaby, and C. V. King. 2008. *Experiencing God: Knowing and Doing the Will of God*. Revised and expanded ed. Nashville: Broadman & Holman.

Blundell, Andrea. 2017. "Your 'Shadow' Self—What It Is, and How It Can Help You." Harley Therapy. https://www.harleytherapy.co.uk/counselling/shadow-self.htm#.

Booker-Drew, F. 2013. "Barriers to Change: Understanding Roadblocks to Progress in Organizations and Communities." Presentation. https://es2.slideshare.net/NonprofitWebinars/barriers-to-change-understanding-roadblocks-to-progress-in-organizations-and-communities.

———. 2014. *From Bonding to Bridging: Using the Immunity to Change (ITC) Process to Build Social Capital and Create Change*. PhD dissertation, Antioch University. https://aura.antioch.edu/etds/144.

———. 2021. "Lamenting Is Necessary for Preservation. All-In-One Integrated Marketing Platform for Small Business." https://mailchi.mp/639a6a19f6d9/lamenting-is-necessary-for-preservation?fbclid=IwAR37lkyAsDp_LSVb4lGrohTFFuiC4Vp259Od2pTpm5_YGrVlfp_WiPwuiS0.

Bourke, J., and A. Titus. 2020. "The Key to Inclusive Leadership." *Harvard Business Review*. https://hbr.org/2020/03/the-key-to-inclusive-leadership.

Brondolo, E., V. Mays, J. S. Jackson, and J. M. Jones. 2019. "Discrimination: What It Is, and How to Cope." American Psychological Association. https://www.apa.org/topics/racism-bias-discrimination/types-stress.

Cáccamo, C. A. 1998. "From 'Switching Code' to 'Code Switching': Towards a Reconceptualisation of Communicative Codes." https://www.academia .edu/971097/From_switching_code_to_code_switching_Towards_a _reconceptualisation_of_communicative_codes.

Carifio, J. 2010. "Development and Validation of a Measure of Relational Leadership: Implications for Leadership Theory and Policies." *Current Research in Psychology* 1. 10.3844/crpsp.2010.16.28.

Center on Budget and Policy Priorities. *Chart Book: SNAP Helps Struggling Families Put Food on the Table.* https://www.cbpp.org/research/food -assistance/chart-book-snap-helps-struggling-families-put-food-on-the -table.

Chandler, J., and K. S. Kennedy. 2015. *A Network Approach to Capacity Building.* National Council of Nonprofits. https://www.councilofnonprofits .org/sites/default/files/documents/a-network-approach-to-capacity -building.pdf.

Cherry, K. 2020. "What Is Cognitive Dissonance?" Verywell Mind. https:// www.verywellmind.com/what-is-cognitive-dissonance-2795012.

Children's Defense Fund. 2021. "The State of America's Children 2020: Child Poverty." https://www.childrensdefense.org/policy/resources/ soac-2020-child-poverty/.

Clark, R. P. 2018. "24 Books for White People to Read beyond Black History Month." The Undefeated. https://theundefeated.com/features/24-books -for-white-people-to-read-beyond-black-history-month/.

Collaborative for Neighborhood Transformation. N.d. "What Is Asset Based Community Development (ABCD)?" ABCD Resources DePaul University. Accessed July 27, 2021. https://resources.depaul.edu/abcd-institute/ resources/Documents/WhatisAssetBasedCommunityDevelopment.pdf.

Connelly, M. 2020. "Kubler-Ross Five Stage Model." *Change Management Coach* (blog). https://www.change-management-coach.com/kubler-ross .html.

Cosby, B. 2004. "Dr. Bill Cosby Speaks at the 50th Anniversary Commemoration of the *Brown v. Topeka Board of Education* Supreme Court Decision, May 22, 2004." *The Black Scholar* 34, no. 4: 2–5. DOI: 10.1080/00064246.2004.11413278.

Da Graca, M., and L. Dougherty. 2015. "Community Cultural Wealth." *First Generation College Students: Navigating Higher Education.* https://scalar .usc.edu/works/first-generation-college-student-/community-cultural -wealth.10.

Dam, A. V. 2019. "The Surprising Holes in Our Knowledge of America's Homeless Population." *Washington Post*. https://www.washingtonpost.com/business/2019/09/18/surprising-holes-our-knowledge-americas-homeless-population/.

Daniel, V. 2019. "Philanthropists Bench Women of Color, the M.V.P.s of Social Change." *New York Times*. https://www.nytimes.com/2019/11/19/opinion/philanthropy-black-women.html.

de Tocqueville, A. 2000. "On the Use That the Americans Make of Association in Civil Life." In *Democracy in America*, translated and edited by H. Mansfield and D. Winthrop, 489-92. Chicago: University of Chicago. https://press.uchicago.edu/Misc/Chicago/805328.html.

DePree, M. 2006. "The Leadership Quest: Three Things Necessary." *Business Strategy Review* 4: 69–74. 10.1111/j.1467-8616.1993.tb00045.x.

Desmond, M. 2018. "Americans Want to Believe Jobs Are the Solution to Poverty. They're Not." *New York Times*. https://www.nytimes.com/2018/09/11/magazine/americans-jobs-poverty-homeless.html.

Dominguez, S., and C. Watkins. 2003. "Creating Networks for Survival and Mobility: Social Capital among African-American and Latin-American Low-Income Mothers." *Social Problems* 50, no. 1: 111–35. https://www.scholars.northwestern.edu/en/publications/creating-networks-for-survival-and-mobility-social-capital-among-.

Dorn, E., B. Hancock, J. Sarakatsannis, and E. Viruleg. 2020. "COVID-19 and Student Learning in the United States: The Hurt Could Last a Lifetime." McKinsey & Company. https://www.mckinsey.com/industries/public-and-social-sector/our-insights/covid-19-and-student-learning-in-the-united-states-the-hurt-could-last-a-lifetime#.

DurhamCares. 2017. "What Is Christian Community Development?" https://durhamcares.org/what-is-christian-community-development/.

The Economist. 2014. "Why Is Everyone So Busy?" https://www.economist.com/news/christmas-specials/21636612-time-poverty-problem-partly-perception-and-partly-distribution-why.

Edwards, A. 2020. "Report: New JLL Snapshot Study Examines How South Dallas Evolved into A Food Desert." Dallas Innovates. https://dallasinnovates.com/report-new-jll-snapshot-study-examines-how-south-dallas-evolved-into-a-food-desert/.

———. 2021. "Southern Dallas County's IPTMA Appoints an Executive Director." Dallas Innovates. https://dallasinnovates.com/southern-dallas-countys-iptma-appoints-an-executive-director/.

Edwards, B., M. W. Foley, and M. Diani. 2002. "Beyond Tocqueville: Civil Society and the Social Capital Debate in Comparative Perspective." *Contemporary Sociology* 31, no. 4: 462-63. 10.2307/3089115.

Eligon, J. 2020. "Black Doctor Dies of Covid-19 after Complaining of Racist Treatment." *New York Times*. https://www.nytimes.com/2020/12/23/us/susan-moore-black-doctor-indiana.html.

FDIC. 2017. *2017 FDIC National Survey of Unbanked and Underbanked Households*. https://www.fdic.gov/analysis/household-survey/2017/2017report.pdf.

Feeding America. N.d. "College Student Hunger Statistics and Research." Retrieved July 27, 2021. https://www.feedingamerica.org/research/college-hunger-research.

Fishbane, L., and A. Tomer. 2020. "As Classes Move Online During COVID-19, What Are Disconnected Students to Do?" *Brookings* (blog). https://www.brookings.edu/blog/the-avenue/2020/03/20/as-classes-move-online-during-covid-19-what-are-disconnected-students-to-do.

Gaiter, J. M. 2016. "Charities, Stop Stereotyping People of Color as Needy." Volunteers of America blog. https://www.voa.org/blog/charities-stop-stereotyping-people-of-color-as-needy.

Giurge, L., and A. Whillans. 2020. *Beyond Material Poverty: Why Time Poverty Matters for Individuals, Organisations, and Nations*. Harvard Business School Working Papers. https://www.hbs.edu/faculty/Pages/item.aspx?num=58352.

Goodman, M. 2016. "Systems Thinking: What, Why, When, Where, and How?" The Systems Thinker. https://thesystemsthinker.com/systems-thinking-what-why-when-where-and-how/.

Graves, Tom. 2014. "RBPEA: On Equality and Gender." *Tetradian* (blog). http://weblog.tetradian.com/2014/11/12/rbpea-on-equality-and-gender/.

Green Doors. N.d. "The Cost of Homelessness Facts." Accessed August 25, 2021. https://www.greendoors.org/facts/cost.php#:~:text=On%20average%2C%20they%20visit%20the,highest%20users%20of%20emergency%20departments.

Greenberg, John. 2017. "10 Examples That Prove White Privilege Exists in Every Aspect Imaginable." *Yes! Magazine*. https://www.yesmagazine.org/social-justice/2017/07/24/10-examples-that-prove-white-privilege-exists-in-every-aspect-imaginable.

Greenleaf, R. K. 1977. *Servant Leadership: A Journey into the Nature of Legitimate Power and Greatness*. Mahwah, N.J.: Paulist Press.

Hains, R. 2019. "Dear Fellow White People: Here's What to Do When You're Called Racist." *Washington Post*. https://www.washingtonpost.com/outlook/dear-fellow-white-people-heres-what-to-do-when-youre-called-racist/2019/08/20/6e31941a-beda-11e9-b873-63ace636af08_story.html.

Harris, I. 2019. "Code-Switching Is Not Trying to Fit in to White Culture, It's Surviving It." *Yes! Magazine*. https://www.yesmagazine.org/opinion/2019/12/17/culture-code-switching.

Hartline-Grafton, H. 2017. "The Impact of Poverty, Food Insecurity, and Poor Nutrition on Health and Well-Being." Food Research and Action Center. https://frac.org/wp-content/uploads/hunger-health-impact-poverty-food-insecurity-health-well-being.pdf.

Haveman, R., and E. N. Wolff. "The Concept and Measurement of Asset Poverty: Levels, Trends and Composition for the U.S., 1983–2001." *Journal of Economic Inequality* 2 (2004): 145–69. https://doi.org/10.1007/s10888-004-4387-3.

Heifetz, R. A., M. Linsky, and A. Grashow. 2009. *The Practice of Adaptive Leadership: Tools and Tactics for Changing Your Organization and the World*. Cambridge, Mass.: Harvard Business Review Press.

Highberger, J. 2020. "Family of 22-Year-Old Who Lost Battle with COVID-19: 'This Is Real.'" NBC 5 Dallas-Fort Worth. https://www.nbcdfw.com/news/coronavirus/family-of-22-year-old-who-lost-battle-with-covid-19-this-is-real/2516227/.

Hoffman, K. M., S. Trawalter, J. R. Axt, and M. N. Oliver. 2016. "Racial Bias in Pain Assessment and Treatment Recommendations, and False Beliefs about Biological Differences between Blacks and Whites." Proceedings of the National Academy of Sciences. https://www.pnas.org/content/113/16/4296.

Holley, J. 2010. "What Is a Network Weaver?" *Network Weaving* (blog). https://networkweaver.blogspot.com/2010/04/what-is-network-weaver.html#.

Horowitz, J. M., A. Brown, and K. Cox. 2019. "Race in America 2019: Public Has Negative Views of the Country's Racial Progress; More Than Half Say Trump Has Made Relations Worse." Pew Research Center. https://www.pewresearch.org/social-trends/2019/04/09/race-in-america-2019/.

HUD. 2019. "HUD 2019 Continuum of Care Homeless Assistance Programs Homeless Populations and Subpopulations." https://files.hudexchange.info/reports/published/CoC_PopSub_NatlTerrDC_2019.pdf.

Infórmate DFW. 2020. "The South Dallas Transportation Initiative." https://informatedfw.com/resources/the-south-dallas-transportation-initiative/.

Institute on Trauma and Trauma-Informed Care. 2015. "What Is Trauma-Informed Care?" Buffalo Center for Social Research, University at Buffalo. https://socialwork.buffalo.edu/social-research/institutes-centers/institute-on-trauma-and-trauma-informed-care/what-is-trauma-informed-care.html.

Jacobs, K., I. E. Perry, and J. MacGillvary. 2015. "The High Public Cost of Low Wages." UC Berkeley Labor Center. https://laborcenter.berkeley.edu/the-high-public-cost-of-low-wages/.

Jaramillo, C. 2017. "Long after College, Divine Nine Fraternities and Sororities Are A Lifeline for Black Members." *Dallas Morning News.* https://www.dallasnews.com/arts-entertainment/2017/11/17/long-after-college-divine-nine-fraternities-and-sororities-are-a-lifeline-for-black-members.

Jensen, Eric. 2009. *Teaching with Poverty in Mind: What Being Poor Does to Kids' Brains and What Schools Can Do about It.* Alexandria, Va.: ASCD.

Jones, J., and W. D. Mosher. 2013. "Fathers' Involvement with Their Children: United States, 2006-2010." *Nation Health Statistics Report* 71. https://www.cdc.gov/nchs/data/nhsr/nhsr071.pdf.

Jordan, J. V. 2000. "The Role of Mutual Empathy in Relational/Cultural Therapy." *Journal of Clinical Psychology* 56, no. 8: 1005-16. https://doi.org/10.1002/1097-4679(200008)56:8<1005::AID-JCLP2>3.0.CO;2-L.

Jordan, J., L. Hartling, and J. Baker. 2008. "The Development of Relational-Cultural Theory." https://www.researchgate.net/publication/247836552_The_Development_of_Relational-Cultural_Theory.

Jordan, J., M. Walker, and L. M. Hartling, eds. 2004. *The Complexity of Connection: Writings from Stone Center's Jean Baker Miller Training Institute.* New York: Guilford Press.

Joseph, E., and B. Winston. 2005. "A Correlation of Servant Leadership, Leader Trust, and Organizational Trust." *Leadership & Organization Development Journal* 26: 6–22. 10.1108/01437730510575552.

The Journal of Blacks in Higher Education. 2018. "The Universities Awarding the Most Doctoral Degrees to Black Scholars." https://www.jbhe.com/2018/12/the-universities-awarding-the-most-doctoral-degrees-to-black-scholars-2/.

Kaiser Family Foundation. 2021. "Distribution of the Nonelderly with Medicaid by Race/Ethnicity." https://www.kff.org/medicaid/state-indicator/distribution-by-raceethnicity-4/?currentTimeframe=0&selectedDistributions=white--black--hispanic--other--total&sortModel=%7B%22colId%22:%22Location%22,%22sort%22:%22asc%22%7D.

Kegan, R., and L. L. Lahey. 2009. *Immunity to Change.* Cambridge, Mass.: Harvard Business Review Press.

The Kirwin Institute. 2012. "Understanding Implicit Bias." The Ohio State University. https://kirwaninstitute.osu.edu/article/understanding-implicit-bias.

Kneebone, E., and N. Holmes. 2016. "The Growing Distance between People and Jobs in Metropolitan America." Brookings. https://www.brookings.edu/research/the-growing-distance-between-people-and-jobs-in-metropolitan-america/.

Kruse, K. 2013. "What Is Leadership?" *Forbes.* https://www.forbes.com/sites/kevinkruse/2013/04/09/what-is-leadership/?sh=548b5ee25b90.

Kübler-Ross, Elisabeth. *On Death and Dying.* New York: Macmillan, 1969.

Laub, James. "Explaining the Servant Mindset: The OLA Servant Leadership Model." Pages 73–112 in *Leveraging the Power of Servant Leadership. Palgrave Studies in Workplace Spirituality and Fulfillment.* Cham, Switzerland: Palgrave Macmillan, 2018. https://doi.org/10.1007/978-3-319-77143-4_4.

Leading Effectively Staff. 2020. "Authentic Leadership: What It Is, Why It Matters." Center for Creative Leadership. https://www.ccl.org/articles/leading-effectively-articles/authenticity-1-idea-3-facts-5-tips/

Lee, T. 2019. "How America's Vast Racial Wealth Gap Grew: By Plunder." *New York Times.* https://www.nytimes.com/interactive/2019/08/14/magazine/racial-wealth-gap.html.

Levine, M. 2019. "Diversifying Boards Means Ceding Control—Are White Nonprofit Leaders Ready?" *Nonprofit Quarterly.* https://nonprofitquarterly.org/diversifying-boards-means-ceding-control-are-white-nonprofit-leaders-ready/.

Linkins, K. W., J. J. Brya, and D. W. Chandler. 2008. *Frequent Users of Health Services Initiative: Final Evaluation Report.* The California Endowment and the California HealthCare Foundation. https://www.aidschicago.org/resources/legacy/pdf/2009/housing_fu_hsinitiative.pdf.

Lipman-Blumen, J. 1992. "CONNECTIVE LEADERSHIP: Female Leadership Styles in the 2lst-Century Workplace." 1992 Pacific Sociological Association. https://assess.connectiveleadership.com/documents/connective_leadership_female_leadership_styles_in_the_21st_century_workplace.pdf.

Lloyd, C. M., S. Anderson, K. Andrews, and D. A. Him. 2021. "Strategies for Building More Equitable Schools When Returning to the Classroom."

Child Trends. https://www.childtrends.org/publications/strategies-for
-building-more-equitable-schools-when-returning-to-the-classroom.

Lumen Learning. N.d. "Cognitive Dissonance." *Introduction to Psychology.*
https://courses.lumenlearning.com/suny-hvcc-psychology-1/chapter/
cognitive-dissonance/#:~:text=What%20is%20Cognitive%20Dissonance
%3F,one%20or%20more%20of%20them.

Martin, J. A., B. E. Hamilton, M. J. K. Osterman, and A. K. Driscoll. 2021.
"Births: Final Data for 2019." *National Vital and Statistics Reports* 70,
no. 2. https://www.cdc.gov/nchs/data/nvsr/nvsr70/nvsr70-02-508.pdf.

Mathie, A., and G. Cunningham. 2003. "From Clients to Citizens: Asset-
Based Community Development." *Development in Practice* 13, no. 5: 474-
86. http://www.jstor.org/stable/4029934.

Mathis, D. T. 2020. "The Church's Black Exodus: Pastor's Silence on Racism and COVID-19 Is Driving Black Parishioners away from Their Congregations." *The Atlantic.* https://www.theatlantic.com/politics/archive/
2020/10/why-black-parishioners-are-leaving-churches/616588/.

McAdams, D. P. 2011. "Narrative Identity." In *Handbook of Identity Theory and
Research*, edited by S. J. Schwartz, K. Luyckx, and V. L. Vignoles, 99–115.
Springer Science + Business Media. https://doi.org/10.1007/978-1-4419
-7988-9_5.

McNulty, M. 2019. "This City Is Paying Homeless People $9.25 an Hour
to Pick Up Street Trash." Fox Business. https://www.foxbusiness.com/
economy/little-rock-homeless-pick-up-trash-payment-program.

Mental Health America. N.d. "Black and African American Communiteis
and Mental Health." https://www.mhanational.org/issues/black-and
-african-american-communities-and-mental-health.

Merkerson, S. E., and R. Metcalf, dirs. 2012. *The Contradictions of
Fair Hope.* Film. New York: Shami Media Group. https://www
.contradictionsoffairhope.com/.

Meyer, L., and I. Floyd. 2020. "Cash Assistance Should Reach Millions More
Families to Lessen Hardship: Families' Access Limited by Policies Rooted in Racism." Center on Budget and Policy Priorities. https://www.cbpp
.org/research/family-income-support/tanf-reaching-few-poor-families.

Moorer, B. 2019. "Seattle Library Program Lets Incarcerated Parents
Read to Their Kids." King5. https://www.king5.com/article/news/
local/seattle-library-read-to-me-program/281-d769c643-3153-4655
-9909-c2c12bbb70b8.

Morin, Amy. 2021. "What Is Cognitive Reframing?" Verywell Mind. https://
www.verywellmind.com/reframing-defined-2610419.

Murphey, D., and P. M. Cooper. 2015. "Parents behind Bars: What Happens to Their Children?" Child Trends. https://www.childtrends.org/wp-content/uploads/2015/10/2015-42ParentsBehindBars.pdf.

Murray, C. 2000. "Deeper into the Brain." Institute for Agriculture & Trade Policy. https://www.iatp.org/sites/default/files/Deeper_into_the_Brain.htm.

Murray, K., and D. Hampton. 2021. "The Connection Between Homelessness and Addiction." Addiction Center. https://www.addictioncenter.com/addiction/homelessness/.

Myers, K. 2019. "US Taxpayers Spent Almost $1 Billion Incarcerating Innocent Black People." Yahoo! Finance. https://finance.yahoo.com/news/us-taxpayers-spent-over-4-billion-incarcerating-innocent-people-184439282.html.

———. 2020. "Racism Has Cost US Economy $16 Trillion in 20 Years: Citi Report." Yahoo! Finance. https://finance.yahoo.com/news/racism-has-cost-us-economy-16-trillion-in-20-years-citi-report-205706392.html.

NAACP. 2021. "Criminal Justice Fact Sheet." https://www.naacp.org/criminal-justice-fact-sheet/.

National Alliance to End Homelessness. 2021. "State of Homelessness: 2020 Edition." https://endhomelessness.org/homelessness-in-america/homelessness-statistics/state-of-homelessness-2020/.

Neitzel, M. T. 2020. "Low Literacy Levels Among U.S. Adults Could Be Costing the Economy $2.2 Trillion a Year." Forbes. https://www.forbes.com/sites/michaeltnietzel/2020/09/09/low-literacy-levels-among-us-adults-could-be-costing-the-economy-22-trillion-a-year/?sh=5c23cee84c90.

Northouse, P. G. 2019. Leadership: Theory and Practice. 8th ed. Thousand Oaks, Calif.: SAGE.

Nova, A. 2019. "The Student Debt Crisis Has Hit Black Students Especially Hard. Here's How." CNBC. https://www.cnbc.com/2019/07/27/how-the-student-debt-crisis-has-hit-black-students-especially-hard.html.

O'Brien, S. 2020. "'I'm Hungry All the Time': How Hunger Has Reached Crisis Level on College Campuses." Yahoo! Life. https://www.yahoo.com/lifestyle/hungry-to-learn-soledad-obrien-investigates-college-student-hunger-crisis-homelessness-035925085.html.

Office of Population Affairs. N.d. "National Teen Pregnancy Prevention Month." U.S. Department of Health and Human Services. Retrieved July 27, 2021. https://opa.hhs.gov/NTPPM.

Oliver, Melvin L., and Thomas M. Shapiro. Black Wealth/White Wealth: A New Perspective on Racial Inequality. New York: Routledge, 1995.

Ollove, M., and C. Vestal. 2020. "COVID-19 Is Crushing Black Communities. Some States Are Paying Attention." The Pew Charitable Trusts. https://www.pewtrusts.org/en/research-and-analysis/blogs/stateline/2020/05/27/covid-19-is-crushing-black-communities-some-states-are-paying-attention.

Onyx, J., M. Edwards, and P. Bullen. 2007. "The Intersection of Social Capital and Power: An Application to Rural Communities." Rural Society 17, no. 3: 215-30. https://doi.org/10.5172/rsj.351.17.3.215.

O'Reilly, B. 2007. "Bill's Comments on Poverty Taken Out of Context." Bill O'Reilly. https://www.billoreilly.com/b/Bills-comments-on-poverty-taken-out-of-context/-717560441766020780.html.

Perrin, A., and E. Turner. 2019. "Smartphones Help Blacks, Hispanics Bridge Some—but Not All—Digital Gaps with Whites." Pew Research Center. https://www.pewresearch.org/fact-tank/2019/08/20/smartphones-help-blacks-hispanics-bridge-some-but-not-all-digital-gaps-with-whites/.

Pew Research Center. 2020a. "Religious Landscape Study: Belief in God." Pew Research Center's Religion & Public Life Project. https://www.pewforum.org/religious-landscape-study/belief-in-god/.

———. 2020b. "Religious Landscape Study: Income Distribution." Pew Research Center's Religion & Public Life Project. https://www.pewforum.org/religious-landscape-study/income-distribution/.

———. 2020c. "Religious Landscape Study: Religions." Pew Research Center's Religion & Public Life Project. https://www.pewforum.org/religious-landscape-study/.

Picardo, E. 2020. "Gentrification." Investopedia. https://www.investopedia.com/terms/g/gentrification.asp.

Pilgrim, D. 2004. "The Truth about the Death of Charles Drew—2004." Jim Crow Museum of Racist Memorabilia. https://www.ferris.edu/HTMLS/news/jimcrow/question/2004/june.htm.

Portman, T., and M. Garrett. 2005. "Beloved Women: Nurturing the Sacred Fire of Leadership from an American Indian Perspective." Journal of Counseling and Development 83: 284–91. 10.1002/j.1556-6678.2005.tb00345.x.

Poverty USA. 2019. "The Population of Poverty USA: Poverty Facts." https://www.povertyusa.org/facts.

Prejean, J. 2021. "Heritage Giving Fund Doubles Its 2021 Grants and Transitions to Moore Impact." My Sweet Charity. https://mysweetcharity.com/2021/03/heritage-giving-fund-doubles-its-2021grants-and-transitions-to-moore-impact/.

Prince, D. N.d. "Laziness Brings Poverty." Derek Prince Ministries USA. https://www.derekprince.org/Articles/1000149861/DPM_USA/ Resources/Word_from_the/Laziness_Brings_Poverty.aspx.

Psychology Today. N.d. "Bias." Accessed July 26, 2021. https://www.psychologytoday.com/us/basics/bias.

Putnam, R. D. 2000. *Bowling Alone: The Collapse and Revival of American Community*. New York: Simon & Schuster.

Queensland University of Technology. 2014. "Don't Bet on Stinginess to Keep Stress Low." ScienceDaily. www.sciencedaily.com/releases/2014/10/141028101625.htm.

Race Forward. 2021. "What Is Racial Equity?" https://www.raceforward.org/about/what-is-racial-equity.

Reid, M. 2019. "This Little Known Fact about Black Giving Might Be Surprising." *Forbes*. https://www.forbes.com/sites/maryannreid/2019/10/30/this-little-known-fact-about-black-giving-might-be-surprising/?sh=416948cb3335.

Renter, E. 2015. "What Generosity Does to Your Brain and Life Expectancy." *U.S. News and World Report*. https://health.usnews.com/health-news/health-wellness/articles/2015/05/01/what-generosity-does-to-your-brain-and-life-expectancy.

Reynolds, J. 2014. "Perceptions of Meritocracy in the Land of Opportunity." *ScienceDirect* 36: 121-37. https://doi.org/10.1016/j.rssm.2014.03.001.

Ritter, Z. 2020. "Polarization May Undermine Community Bonds, Trust in Others." Gallup. https://news.gallup.com/opinion/gallup/284357/polarization-may-undermine-community-bonds-trust-others.aspx.

Robertson, C. 2018. "A Quiet Exodus: Why Black Worshipers Are Leaving White Evangelical Churches." *New York Times*. https://www.nytimes.com/2018/03/09/us/blacks-evangelical-churches.html.

Ross, J. 2019. "As McConnell's Family Shows, the Legacy of Slavery Persists in Most American Lives." NBC News. https://www.nbcnews.com/news/nbcblk/mcconnell-s-family-shows-legacy-slavery-persists-most-american-lives-n1028031.

Sacerdote, B. 2002. "Slavery and the Intergenerational Transmission of Human Capital." National Bureau of Economic Resource Working Papers. https://www.nber.org/papers/w9227.

Schön, D. A. 1987. *Educating the Reflective Practitioner: Toward a New Design for Teaching and Learning in the Professions*. San Francisco: Jossey-Bass.

Schott Foundation. 2012. "Opportunity Gap—Key Data." http://schottfoundation.org/issues/opportunity-gap/key-organizations.

Schwartz, K. 2019. "How Ibram X. Kendi's Definition of Antiracism Applies to Schools." KQED. https://www.kqed.org/mindshift/54999/how-ibram-x-kendis-definition-of-antiracism-applies-to-schools.

Seales, C. 2018. "That Blacks Are Leaving White Churches Should Surprise Nobody. Here Is What to Do about It." UT News. https://news.utexas.edu/2018/05/17/what-to-do-about-blacks-leaving-white-churches/.

The Sentencing Project. 2018. "Report to the United Nations on Racial Disparities in the U.S. Criminal Justice System." https://www.sentencingproject.org/publications/un-report-on-racial-disparities/.

Senters, K. 2018. "Heritage Giving Fund at Dallas Women's Foundation Hosts Powerful Philanthropy Discussion." Texas Women's Foundation. https://txwf.org/heritage-giving-fund-at-dallas-womens-foundation-hosts-powerful-philanthropy-discussion/.

Shinneman, S. 2019. "Two Dallas ZIP Codes Produce More Inmates Than Any Others in Texas." *D Magazine.* https://www.dmagazine.com/frontburner/2019/11/two-dallas-zip-codes-produce-more-inmates-than-any-others-in-texas/.

Siefker, K. N.d. "NAACP Youth Council Picket Line, 1955 Texas State Fair." The Story of Texas. Retrieved July 27, 2021. https://www.thestoryoftexas.com/discover/artifacts/naacp-state-fair-spotlight-012315#:%7E:text=In%201955%2C%20the%20Texas%20State,Negro%20Achievement%20Day%20in%201936.

Simpson, Joanna. *Everyone Belongs: A Toolkit for Applying Intersectionality*, June 2009. Canadian Research Institute for the Advancement of Women (CRIAW). http://www.disabilitystudies.ca/assets/ccds-int-dis--151110-final-report-en-full.pdf.

Smith, J. M. 2014. "Want to Be Happy? Stop Being So Cheap!" *New Republic.* https://newrepublic.com/article/119477/science-generosity-why-giving-makes-you-happy.

Smith, L. T. 2012. *Decolonizing Methodologies: Research and Indigenous Peoples.* 2nd edition. London: Zed Books.

Smooth W. G. 2013. "Intersectionality from Theoretical Framework to Policy Intervention." In *Situating Intersectionality*, edited by A. R. Wilson, 11–41. New York: Palgrave Macmillan. https://doi.org/10.1057/9781137025135_2.

Somin, A. 2015. "Eminent Domain and Race." *The Federalist Society* (blog). https://fedsoc.org/commentary/fedsoc-blog/eminent-domain-and-race.

Stat, T. Y. 2015. "Be Generous: It's a Simple Way to Stay Healthier." *Chicago Tribune.* https://www.chicagotribune.com/lifestyles/health/sc-hlth-0812-joy-of-giving-20150806-story.html.

Statistical Atlas. 2018. "Race and Ethnicity in South Dallas, Dallas, Texas." https://statisticalatlas.com/neighborhood/Texas/Dallas/South-Dallas/Race-and-Ethnicity.

Stearn, R. 2018. "The Power of a Broken Heart." World Vision Churches blog. https://church.worldvision.org/blog/_bloq_blog_articles/the-power-of-a -broken-heart/12?article=true.

Stephens, J. 2020. "The United States of Accents: African American Vernacular English." Babbel Magazine. https://www.babbel.com/en/magazine/african-american-vernacular-english.

Stewart, D. 2020. "As a Black Person, I'm Done Helping White Christians Feel Better about Race." *Washington Post*. https://www.washingtonpost.com/outlook/2020/07/13/black-pastor-white-churches/.

Terrion, J. L. 2006. "The Development of Social Capital through A Leadership Training Program." *MountainRise: The International Journal for the Scholarship of Teaching and Learning* 3, no. 2. http://hdl.handle.net/10393/22767.

Thomas-Breitfeld, S. 2017. "Aspiring Nonprofit Leaders of Color Face Structural Bias, Study Finds." Philanthropy News Digest. https://philanthropynewsdigest.org/news/aspiring-nonprofit-leaders-of-color -face-structural-bias-study-finds.

Thomas-Breitfeld, S., and F. Kunreuther. 2019. *Nonprofit Executives and the Racial Leadership Gap: A Race to Lead Brief*. Building Movement Project. https://www.buildingmovement.org/wp-content/uploads/2019/07/ED .CEO_Race_to_Lead_Brief_.pdf.

Tilly, C. 1998. *Durable Inequality*. Berkeley: University of California Press.

The Times Editorial Board. 2018. "Editorial: A Job Picking up Trash Won't Pull a Homeless Person Off the Street. But It's Not a Bad Start." *Los Angeles Times*. https://www.latimes.com/opinion/editorials/la-ed-homeless -trash-pickup-20181120-story.html.

Tozier, D. 2019. "Union Station Homeless Services Remains Committed to Helping Community Members Despite Obstacles." *Pasadena Magazine*. https://pasadenamag.com/people-places/community/union-station -homeless-services-remains-committed-to-helping-community-members -despite-obstacles/.

Tyko, K. 2019. "Billionaire Robert F. Smith's $34 Million Gift to Morehouse Grads Includes Parent Loans." *USA Today*. https://usatoday.com/story/money/2019/09/20/morehouse-billionaire-gift-smith-donates-34 -million-pay-off-loans/2392458001/.

U.S. Bureau of Labor Statistics. 2019. *A Profile of the Working Poor, 2017.* BLS Reports. https://www.bls.gov/opub/reports/working-poor/2017/home.htm.

Understand Together. N.d. "Community Assets." https://www.understandtogether.ie/Get-involved/Community-activation/Community%20assets%20analysis.pdf.

USDA ERS. 2021. "About the Atlas." https://www.ers.usda.gov/data-products/food-access-research-atlas/about-the-atlas/.

Vaid, U., and A. Maxton. 2017. *The Apparitional Donor: Understanding and Engaging High Net Worth Donors of Color.* New York: The Advancement Project and The Vaid Group LLC. https://www.donorsofcolor.org/wp-content/uploads/2019/01/FinalAppDonreport4.17.pdf.

Vaughn, J. 2020. "City Says It Found Money to Clean Up Shingle Mountain, but Doubts Persist." *Dallas Observer.* https://www.dallasobserver.com/news/dallas-says-it-will-pay-to-remove-shingle-mountain-11941505.

Villarosa, L. 2019. "How False Beliefs in Physical Racial Difference Still Live in Medicine Today." *New York Times.* https://www.nytimes.com/interactive/2019/08/14/magazine/racial-differences-doctors.html.

VoyageDallas. 2017. "Meet Akilah Wallace of HERitage Giving Fund in Dallas." http://voyagedallas.com/interview/meet-akilah-wallace-heritage-giving-fund-dallas/.

Walker, M., and W. B. Rosen, eds. 2004. *How Connections Heal: Stories from Relational-Cultural Therapy.* New York: Guilford Press.

West, C. M. 2017. "Mammy, Sapphire, Jezebel, and the Bad Girls of Reality Television: Media Representations of Black Women." In *Lectures on the Psychology of Women*, edited by J. Chrisler and C. Golden, 5th ed., 139–58. Long Grove, Ill.: Waveland Press.

Wetzel, J., and C. Ward. 2020. "Jobs Market Is Struggling, and the Formerly Incarcerated Are Being Prevented from Helping." *USA Today.* https://www.usatoday.com/story/opinion/policing/2020/02/20/jobs-market-struggling-formerly-incarcerated-being-prevented-helping/4785607002/.

Wheatley, M. J. 1992. *Leadership and the New Science: Learning about Organization from an Orderly Universe.* Oakland: Berrett-Koehler Publishers.

Wigglesworth, V. 2012. "The Burden of Lead: West Dallas Deals with Contamination Decades Later." Dallas Morning News. https://www.dallasnews.com/news/2012/12/15/the-burden-of-lead-west-dallas-deals-with-contamination-decades-later/.

Women's Philanthropy Institute. 2019. *Women Give 2019: Gender and Giving Across Communities of Color.* Indiana University Lilly Family School of Philanthropy. https://scholarworks.iupui.edu/bitstream/handle/1805/18629/women-give2019-1.pdf

Worth, D. N. 2020. "Cleanup at Southern Dallas' 'Shingle Mountain' Set to Begin." NBC 5 Dallas-Fort Worth. https://www.nbcdfw.com/news/local/cleanup-at-southern-dallas-shingle-mountain-set-to-begin/2504903/.

Yosso, Tara J. "Whose Culture Has Capital?" *Race, Ethnicity and Education* 8, no. 1 (2005): 69–91.

Young, M. 2001. "Down with Meritocracy." *The Guardian.* https://www.theguardian.com/politics/2001/jun/29/comment.

Youth.gov. N.d. "Children of Incarcerated Parents: The Impact of Incarceration." https://youth.gov/sites/default/files/COIPInfographic_508.pdf.

YW Boston. 2017. "What Is Intersectionality, and What Does It Have to Do with Me?" YW Boston blog. https://www.ywboston.org/2017/03/what-is-intersectionality-and-what-does-it-have-to-do-with-me/.

Zacharakis, J., and J. Flora. 2005. "Riverside: A Case Study of Social Capital and Cultural Reproduction and Their Relationship to Leadership Development." *Adult Education Quarterly* 55, no. 4: 288-307.

Zauzmer, J. 2019. "Christians Are More Than Twice As Likely to Blame a Person's Poverty on Lack of Effort." *Washington Post.* https://www.washingtonpost.com/news/acts-of-faith/wp/2017/08/03/christians-are-more-than-twice-as-likely-to-blame-a-persons-poverty-on-lack-of-effort.

RESOURCES

This list is not comprehensive but can serve as a guide. In addition, you can find more resources in the reference section.

Race In America

Various

Anti-Racist Resources for Self-Care for BIPOCs
https://projects.iq.harvard.edu/antiracismresources/bipoc/selfcare

"First, Listen. Then, Learn: Anti-Racism Resources for White People"
https://www.forbes.com/sites/juliawuench/2020/06/02/first-listen-then
-learn-anti-racism-resources-for-white-people/

National Council of Churches Anti-Racist Resource Guide
https://nationalcouncilofchurches.us/anti-racism-resources/

Books and Articles

10 Books about Race to Read Instead of Asking a POC to Explain It to
You https://diversity.uconn.edu/10-books-to-read-about-race/

75 Things White People Can Do for Racial Justice
https://csis.upenn.edu/independent-learning/75-things-white-people
-can-do-for-racial-justice/

Anti-Racism Resources for BIPOCs
https://projects.iq.harvard.edu/antiracismresources/bipoc/reading

Be the Bridge: Pursuing God's Heart for Racial Reconciliation, by Latasha
Morrison
https://latashamorrison.com/book/

Facing Racism: A Vision of the Intercultural Community—Antiracism Study Guides, PCUSA
https://facing-racism.pcusa.org/site_media/media/uploads/facing
_racism/facing-racism-study-guide.pdf

How to Fight Racism: Courageous Christianity and the Journey Toward Racial Justice, by Jemar Tisby
https://www.zondervan.com/9780310104773/how-to-fight-racism/

Study Guides for Racism, Baylor University
https://www.baylor.edu/content/services/document.php/110990.pdf

"White Privilege: Unpacking the Invisible Knapsack," by Peggy McIntosh
https://nationalseedproject.org/Key-SEED-Texts/white-privilege
-unpacking-the-invisible-knapsack

Videos and Podcasts

Code Switch
https://www.npr.org/podcasts/510312/codeswitch

"How to Be an Anti-Racist": Interview with Dr. Ibram X. Kendi
https://www.youtube.com/watch?v=TzuOlyyQlug

Intersectionality Matters
https://podcasts.apple.com/us/podcast/intersectionality-matters/
id1441348908

Pod for the Cause
https://civilrights.org/podforthecause/

Race, Justice and the Church
https://www.rightnowmedia.org/content/series/420440

Seeing White
https://www.sceneonradio.org/seeing-white/

United Shades of America, by W. Kamau Bell
https://www.cnn.com/shows/united-shades-of-america

Organizations and Initiatives

1619 Project
https://www.nytimes.com/interactive/2019/08/14/magazine/1619
-america-slavery.html

Anti-Defamation League
https://www.adl.org/

Race Forward
https://www.raceforward.org/

Jack and Jill of America
https://www.jackandjillinc.org/

The Links, Incorporated
https://linksinc.org/

National Pan-Hellenic Council (Divine Nine)
https://nphchq.com/millennium1/

Southern Poverty Law Center
https://www.splcenter.org/

Talking about Race
https://nmaahc.si.edu/learn/talking-about-race

While I Have Your Attention
https://www.wfaa.com/article/news/local/outreach/while-i-have-your
-attention/while-i-have-your-attention/287-02028aff-96ae-4a9c-a21c
-991aeb359f9d

Networks/Social Capital

The Network Weaver Handbook: A Guide to Transformational Networks,
by June Holley
https://networkweaver.com/product/network-weaver-handbook-pdf/

Bowling Alone: The Collapse and Revival of American Community, by
Robert D. Putnam
http://bowlingalone.com/

Giving Circles and Philanthropy

How to Start a Giving Circle
https://www.givingtuesday.org/blog/2019/10/give-better-together-how
-start-or-join-giving-circle

Learning to Give
https://www.learningtogive.org/resources

The Miseducation of Black Philanthropy
https://www.tides.org/accelerating-social-change/philanthropy

Asset-Based Community Development and Christian Community Development

Asset-Based Community Development
https://resources.depaul.edu/abcd-institute/Pages/default.aspx

Beyond Charity: The Call for Christian Community Development, by John Perkins
http://bakerpublishinggroup.com/books/beyond-charity/142920

Faith and Leadership: John McKnight on ABCD
https://faithandleadership.com/john-mcknight-low-income
-communities-are-not-needy-they-have-assets

Nurture Development: Asset-Based Community Development
https://www.nurturedevelopment.org/asset-based-community
-development/

"Resources for Churches on Asset-Based Community Development"
https://sustainingcommunity.wordpress.com/2018/09/20/abcd-churches/

Leadership

Authentic Leadership

"Managing Authenticity: The Paradox of Great Leadership"
https://hbr.org/2005/12/managing-authenticity-the-paradox-of-great
-leadership

"What Is Authentic Leadership?"
https://www.forbes.com/sites/kevinkruse/2013/05/12/what-is-authentic
-leadership/?sh=3e6e0ccadef7

Relational Leadership

"Now More Than Ever, We Need Relational Leadership"
https://accelerate.uofuhealth.utah.edu/connect/now-more-than-ever-we
-need-relational-leadership

"What Is the Relational Leadership Model?"
https://www.graduateprogram.org/2020/09/what-is-the-relational
-leadership-model/

Inclusive Leadership

"Inclusive Leadership: Steps Your Organization Should Take to Get it Right"
https://www.ccl.org/articles/leading-effectively-articles/when-inclusive
-leadership-goes-wrong-and-how-to-get-it-right/

"The Key to Inclusive Leadership"
https://hbr.org/2020/03/the-key-to-inclusive-leadership

"What Is Inclusive Leadership?"
https://resources.workable.com/what-is-inclusive-leadership#

Organizations to Know

ABCD Institute
https://resources.depaul.edu/abcd-institute/Pages/default.aspx

Black Philanthropy Month
http://www.blackphilanthropymonth.com/

Buckner International
https://www.buckner.org

Christian Community Development Association
https://ccda.org

Faith In Action
https://faithinaction.org

Give 8/28
https://www.give828.org/giving-events/ybgb20

Giving Tuesday
https://hq.givingtuesday.org

Grantmakers for Girls of Color
https://www.grantmakersforgirlsofcolor.org

HERitage Giving Fund
https://www.heritagegivingfund.org

Kellogg Truth, Racial Healing, and Transformation
https://healourcommunities.org

List of South Dallas nonprofits
https://servesouthdallas.org

Mission Waco (Poverty Simulation)
https://missionwaco.org

Philanthropy Together
https://philanthropytogether.org

Power In Action
https://www.mightycause.com/organization/Wearepiadallas

The Wise Fund
https://thewisefund.org/

Women of Color in Fundraising and Philanthropy
https://www.woc-fp.com

World Vision U.S. Programs
https://www.worldvision.org/our-work/country-profiles/united-states

BIOGRAPHY OF
DR. FROSWA' BOOKER-DREW

Froswa' Booker-Drew, PhD is a Network Weaver who believes relationships are the key to our personal, professional and organizational growth. She has been quoted/featured in *Forbes*, Ozy, Bustle, Huffington Post, Modern Luxury, and other media outlets, due to an extensive background in leadership, nonprofit management, philanthropy, partnership development, training, and education. She is currently Vice President of Community Affairs for the State Fair of Texas, responsible for grant-making, educational programming, and community initiatives. Formerly the National Community Engagement Director for World Vision, she served as a catalyst, partnership broker, and builder of the capacity of local partners in multiple locations across the United States to improve and sustain the well-being of children and their families. She is also cofounder for HERitage Giving Circle, one of the first Black women's giving circles in the state of Texas, founder of Power in Action Dallas, and the owner of Soulstice Consultancy, which provides training and consultations for nonprofits and small businesses.

Dr. Booker-Drew was a part of the documentary *Friendly Captivity*, a film that follows a cast of seven women from Dallas to India. She is the recipient of several honors including 2020 Each Moment Matters Awardee, 2020 Dallas Leadership Foundation's Leadership Award, WFAA's While I Have Your Attention (2020), 2020 TEDxSMU speaker, 2019 *Dallas Business Journal's* Women in Business honoree, Alpha Kappa Alpha, Inc. Global Big Heart 2014, 2012 Outstanding African American Alumni Award from the University of Texas at Arlington, 2009 Woman of the Year Award by Zeta Phi Beta Sorority, Inc., and Diversity Ambassador for the American Red Cross (2012).

Froswa' graduated with a PhD from Antioch University's School of Leadership and Change with a focus on social capital, diverse women, change management, and relational leadership. She attended the Jean Baker Miller Institute at Wellesley for training in Relational Cultural Theory and has completed facilitator training on Immunity to Change based on the work of Kegan and Lahey of Harvard. She has also completed training through UNICEF on Equity-Focused Evaluations. Booker-Drew is currently an adjunct professor at Tulane University in the Master of Public Administration Program teaching a course on Governance, Leadership, and Sustainability. She was awarded 2021 Distinguished Faculty Member for the program and serves as an affiliate faculty member at the Graduate School of Leadership and Change, Antioch University. She has also been an adjunct professor at the University of North Texas at Dallas, the University of Texas at Arlington, and Capital Seminary and Graduate School. She is the host of the podcast *The Tapestry* and author of three workbooks for women: *Fly Away*, *Ready for a Revolution: 30 Days to Jolt Your Life*, and *Rules of Engagement: Making Connections Last*. Froswa' serves on multiple boards including Buckner International, For Oak Cliff, EdCor, Mayor's Star Council, and Soul Rep Theater Company. She was a workshop presenter at the United Nations in 2013 on Access to Power. She has been a contributor for several publications globally, including as an advice columnist for professional women at Business Woman Media, a global platform based in Australia.

CPSIA information can be obtained
at www.ICGtesting.com
Printed in the USA
LVHW040724180523
747321LV00002B/133

9 781481 316095